The

to College

Volume Two

Greg Swinney, editor

Lifechange Media
Kearney, NE

LIFECHANGE MEDIA

Library of Congress Cataloging-in-Publication Data

Swinney, Greg
The Gospel Goes to College – Volume 2
ISBN 978-0-9852128-5-8
Christian life. I Title. I. Ministry

First printing: January 2021

Cover design: Lifechange Media
www.Lifechange-Media.com

Printed in the United States of America by
Morris Publishing®
3212 East Highway 30
Kearney, NE 68847
1-800-650-7888

With Gratitude for...

Each of the contributors to this work wish to express their gratitude:

I thank God for sending Lynn Harris to me. She has been the best wife I could imagine or ask for. She loves Jesus fully and completely, believing every word He spoke. *(Mark Pike)*

I am grateful for God's patience and kindness, grace and tenacity on this journey and for the collective wisdom and love expressed in and through our family, awesome staff, and decades of Jesus-following Boilermakers. *(Rob Schrumpf)*

I'm profoundly grateful for Joy, my partner in life and ministry. We met in college ministry, got engaged after our Tuesday evening student gathering, and honeymooned at a college ministry leadership conference. We treasure the students we've encountered along the way, and we are blessed to have two students of our own, Aaron and Ethan. *(Matt Stafford)*

Special thanks to my brother, Greg, without whom I would be missing an entire dimension of my life – rich, lifelong friendships with international students and many of their families. Being first, part of the Christian Student Fellowship campus ministry team, and now part of the Crossroads International Ministry has been a blessing beyond words. Thank you for your continual support and fervent prayers on this lifelong spiritual journey. *(Cindy Swinney)*

My heartfelt gratitude goes to the board of Directors of Christian Campus House for their tireless efforts of serving alongside me, the students who have inspired me and gone on to do wonderful things for God's Kingdom, and especially my family, who have lived their lives in "collegeland" through no fault of their own. *(Dave Embree)*

I love campus ministry and university students. I am indebted to those students in my ministries at Oklahoma State University and Eastern Illinois University from whom I learned so much in 38 years. Together we planned, toiled, laughed, wept, and grew. Without their "iron sharpening iron" influence in my life, I would not have grown into the person God has made me. But my greatest debt is owed to my wife, Sue, with whom I have shared life's pilgrimage and ministry's challenges and blessings. *(Roger Songer)*

I would like to thank my wife, Christi, and our three boys for being extremely flexible during our years serving in campus ministry. Many late nights, long weekends, and countless nights away on the road were accepted with much grace. In addition, they all were invaluable in helping our family, and our ministry develop a culture of appreciation and purpose surrounding international student ministry. It was my wife who told me I should cancel my original plans for research and refocus those plans on international student ministry. If it had not been for her, this chapter would never have been written. Thank you to my wife for that push, and all the other time you push me in the right direction to be a better kingdom servant, father and husband. *(Barry Reed)*

I wish to thank the hundreds of students and professors who inspired me by leaving all for Truth and Love, Jesus Christ. Deep thanks to my father and mother who showed me "only what's done for Christ will last"; and to Garland Bare, Roy Weece, and Gary Hawes, who taught me so much about campus ministry.

Special thanks to my wife Carol who daily shows, "It is more blessed to give than to receive." *(Dr. Bob Milliken)*

Visionary leaders through the years have impacted my life in transformational ways. People like Jerry Arnold Jr., and his Dad, Gerald, Ed Hackel and his family, David Empson, Clark Bates and Jerry Hopkins, and so many more in leadership. I'm thankful for the encouraging phone calls from Hari and Christy, and for the notes from countless numbers of people around the world.

I don't know what I did to deserve friends like all of you. Thank you for your love and patience for someone like me who is a work in progress as I'm continually shaped by the Master's Hand. *(Greg Swinney)*

Preface
Volume Two

He waved at me from across the room and walked in my direction. Although he was nearly eighty years old, the spring in his step made him seem like he was only fifty. His white hair gave him a dignified look and his gentle smile seemed welcoming as he introduced himself to me. *"Hello, I'm Doug Dickey and I hear you are from Nebraska,"* he said with a grin. From that time on our friendship blossomed over the next ten years.

Doug included me.

Across the room in that same meeting was another white-haired fella that people described as having *"the voice of God."* I sat next to Roy Weece during that meeting and felt like I should take notes on our conversation. His eyes, filled with compassion, told stories without saying a word. He asked how I was and offered to help in any way he could.

Roy inspired me.

A few years later, a balding guy with a contagious smile, round glasses and a huge tattoo on his left ankle grinned and asked me to tell him my story. After muttering a few words, I realized this was Ward Patterson. The guy who rode a motorcycle through much of Asia and wrote books that I found fascinating. He asked me to help him teach a campus ministry class at Purdue University that summer. That was like asking a gorilla to play a violin in his symphony orchestra. Of course, I said yes.

Ward involved me.

Through the years, I have been blessed with mentors who didn't see me for what I was or where I was from, but for who I could become. Never once did the thought cross my mind, *"what do these old geezers know..."* Instead, I saw them as pioneers, risk-takers, trendsetters, and friends. I couldn't wait to have my feet under the same table as them. Today, I feel as though I ride on their shoulders.

This second Volume of the Gospel Goes to College is written by godly people who want to include you, inspire you and involve you. These writers are visionary leaders who have sacrificed so much to humbly accept the calling of "Campus Minister." I've spent time with each of these authors and I can say without reservation, they set an amazing example of godly leadership. We can learn so much from them.

Now that I'm in my sixties I occasionally get referred to as being "an old guy." One of the privileges of being "old" is that one can give advice. No one may pay any attention, but that doesn't stop us from giving it.

After nearly four decades in active campus ministry, I've learned a lot. Mostly from mistakes, but nevertheless, I've learned. As a newbie to the campus, I needed help. Now, after many years of serving, I often find myself stuck. Students are different these days, the culture has changed.

I've changed. Pandemics come and reset the table. I still need help.

These eleven writers are giving us just that – practical, inspirational, common sense – help.

This book can help you become the leader God intends you to be in the place where He has put you. Psalm 78:72 describes David as one leading with integrity and skill. May this book help you in your quest to do the same.

Greg Swinney
Kearney, NE
2021

Contents

Chapter 1

DEVELOPING AN EFFECTIVE CAMPUS MINISTRY BOARD OF DIRECTORS

By Mark Pike

Have you ever been in a situation where the last thing you wanted to attend was a board meeting? Would you like for the board of your ministry to be a dynamic force rather than an energy drain?

Leadership boards must be an effective resource for your ministry, your organization, your church. The right people, key Biblical principles, time and work all make a world of difference in the long run. There are no free lunches or shortcuts to an effective board and staff leadership.

Important Biblical principles are the best place to begin and looking at the stories of Rehoboam and Moses offers helpful direction.

The Folly of Rehoboam

After 40 years, the reign of King Solomon thudded to a stop. The spectacle at the end was quite different than the promise of wisdom and splendor which marked his initial years as king. In 1 Kings 11 & 12, the chronicler of Israel's kings reported that the legacy of Solomon was sullied by devotion to pagan cults, the influence of foreign wives and practices which were evil in the sight of God. He became a very different king than his father David.

Israel looked to Rehoboam to restore the glory of his grandfather's throne and the aborted potential of his father's reign. At his coronation, on the hill of Shechem, as the people of Israel gathered to make him king, Rehoboam had the chance to chart a new course. The leaders of Israel asked him to lighten the heavy yoke of his father and lower the burden of heavy taxation. If he did this, they would serve him as their king. Rehoboam spent three days considering their request.

Rehoboam sought the counsel of two groups of advisors. He consulted with the old men who had served with Solomon. These men who had advised Solomon gave Rehoboam a surprising answer. Serve the people, give them a favorable response and they will serve you forever. Their experience of watching Solomon was invaluable.

Next, he consulted the young men with whom he had grown up. The friends of Rehoboam had something different in mind to suggest to the king. They advised him to say to the people: *"My little finger is thicker than my father's thighs. And now, whereas my father laid on you a heavy yoke, I will add to your yoke. My father disciplined you with whips, but I will discipline you with scorpions."* They certainly knew how to turn a memorable phrase evoking the power of a tyrant rather than a Hebrew shepherd king.

Rehoboam preferred the advice of his friends over the wisdom offered by the elders. When the nation heard the response of the king, they turned from him. The Bible says that Israel, "went to their tents" which is a poetic way of saying that Rehoboam and the tribe of Judah were on their own. The nation was plunged into rebellion and division.

There are some important lessons to learn from the experience of Rehoboam. But, to gain an even broader perspective another story is important to consider. The account of Moses and Jethro (Exodus 18) tells of a leader accepting advice from an elder and the outcome is remarkable.

The Wisdom of Jethro

Moses and Israel witnessed the mighty power of God firsthand. He redeemed Israel from their slavery in Egypt and delivered them from the oppressive Pharaoh. He provided bread and water during the wilderness journey to Sinai. But now the glow of triumph was beginning to wear thin as the reality of leading a large group of people consumed the time and attention of Moses. In Exodus 18:13 we read that the people of Israel *"stood about Moses from the morning until the evening"* to inquire of God and settle their disputes. Moses may have had thoughts of returning to the shepherding business as he listened to their quarrels.

Fortunately, for Moses, he received a visit from his father-in-law, Jethro. After the greetings and blessings were exchanged, Jethro noticed what Moses was doing and how he was using his time judging the people. Jethro told Moses that this work was too heavy a load to carry alone, that he would not be able to do it. He gave Moses some sound advice about understanding and ordering this work.

Jethro reminded Moses to keep the main responsibility the first thing.

First, Jethro reminded Moses that his primary task was to teach the people, to help them understand "the way in which they must walk and what they must do." Moses had the responsibility to teach the ways of God to the people and he was not able to fulfill that task as long as he was settling disputes day and night. Jethro reminded Moses to keep the main responsibility the first thing.

Second, Jethro instructed Moses to *"look for able men from all the people, men who fear God, who are trustworthy and hate a bribe"* to help him carry the load of judging the people. Moses was to share the work of leading the people with the people themselves. Jethro, the desert sheik, told Moses to share leadership and responsibility. This is an important principle of ministry leadership which we will consider more fully in the next section.

Third, Jethro instructed Moses to organize the leaders into a hierarchy of authority and responsibility. The able men were to be "chiefs of thousands, of hundreds, of fifties, and of tens." The work would be grouped into manageable tasks and the leaders had the authority to help Moses with judging the people.

The moment of decision came. Moses could have reacted to Jethro by saying something like, *"Who are you to give me advice? I have been with these people for a long time and I know what I am doing."* But Moses did not do that. He listened to Jethro and implemented his ideas. The Bible closes this story with the following observation: *"Then Moses let his father-in-law depart, and he went away to his own country."*

Biblical Principles for an Effective Board

You might wonder what the stories of Rehoboam and Moses have to do with dry, dusty board meetings. Or, maybe your experience with boards has led you to view them as a necessary evil and an irrelevant distraction from your real work. Several principles emerge in these stories to help a board of directors function in a healthy manner. Practical wisdom helps head off the dullness experienced in some board meetings and even helps you to view your board differently. There is transformational influence through an effective board.

Serve the people and they will serve you

It raises the question of who are the people we serve, whose consent empowers our leadership? The first answer is students. Several important ministry dynamics flow from this fact. A campus ministry must connect with students in ways that connect them with God. Students must engage in worship, prayer, Bible study, service, mission and leadership development. I think of this as the blocking and tackling of campus ministry, the basics.

This engagement with students is also crucial for the campus minister. An effective campus minister must connect with students. He or she must enjoy working with students and they must enjoy working with the campus minister. We know this to be campus ministry 101. But it is not enough.

Without an effective board our vision narrows.

The answer to the question of the people we serve cannot be only the students currently in our ministry. The people we serve include alumni, students on campus but not in our ministry, donors, supporting churches, and the university community. This is where our board comes into play. An effective board helps us see the big picture of all the people we serve.

Without an effective board our vision narrows, often to ministry with the people we like the most, our friends.

When that happens, we forget the scope of our mission, the history of our ministry and the future God is leading us toward. Just as Israel did not exist only for herself or her king, but for all the families of the earth, a healthy campus ministry exists for more people than the students involved this semester. In the next section on the practices of an effective board, we will consider some steps to help our board reflect all the people we serve in ways that empower our ministry.

Listen to your Advisors not just your Friends

Because Rehoboam did not understand his relationship with Israel he did not listen to his advisors. Because Moses did understand his mission, he listened to his advisor, even when it came from a source outside the nation of Israel in the person of Jethro the Midianite.

Understanding the people we serve will focus and empower our listening. In both the story of Rehoboam and the story of Moses, the Bible emphasizes taking into account the whole nation, all the people for a reason. Jesus taught us the importance of listening: "He that has ears to hear, let him hear" is one of the memorable phrases in his teaching.

When our board was going through the process of reviewing and updating our Bylaws, one of our alumni who is the pastor of a supporting church and a member of our Ministerial Advisor board expressed his objections. I remember the morning he called me to voice his opposition and the possibility of his church withdrawing support from the ministry. It was the morning after our first Sunday worship service of the Fall Semester. We had just welcomed 150 students to our ministry. We had a long list of students to contact and at this crucial moment, my friend was calling to cancel his support. I wanted to get to work, contacting those students and get our student leaders organized. That was not the best time to be distracted by dealing with an unhappy advisor.

Because I valued our relationship with this pastor and alumnus, I spent some time reflecting on his concerns before responding. Had we missed something in our deliberations on the Bylaws? I called a few of our Board members, told them of the phone call, listened to their perspectives. A few days later I called my friend and set a breakfast meeting to discuss his concerns and consider ways to mend the relationship.

When we met we discussed his concerns. I assured him that the Board viewed the new Bylaws as a document that would need to be reviewed regularly. Could we take up his concerns at a future meeting and consider them at that time? By the time we were having this conversation, it was only two weeks from an announced meeting for supporting churches to vote on approval of the final form of the Bylaws. These had previously been approved by the Board. He somewhat agreed with our reasoning, but wanted to think about it further and discuss the matter again with the chair of his missions committee.

The next day I called the pastor. He was ready to drop all his objections and the church would continue their support of the ministry. What had changed? We had talked and we had respectfully listened to each other. We took the time necessary and we valued each other. It helped that my friend had received a letter from his church's insurance company encouraging them to amend their Bylaws to address similar issues that our board had addressed.

Listen to all your advisors, even if it takes extra time and work.

Keep your mission in mind

The first piece of advice for Moses from Jethro is instructive. Moses was spending too much time settling disputes and it was taking time from his teaching the word of God. Moses needed to protect his time and focus on his teaching role among the people so they would know how to conduct their lives in light of God's ways.

Understanding the mission of your campus ministry and your role in pursuing that mission is critical. It is also a matter of discernment that we cannot do alone. I was called to our ministry by our board; they set the initial terms of my calling at the Christian Student Foundation. Their input is vital to the continuing effectiveness of our ministry.

Their input is vital to the continuing effectiveness of our ministry.

The truth is I need help with keeping the mission the main thing. I can drift into doing what I prefer to do: meeting with the people I enjoy, reading the books I like and occasionally avoiding difficult tasks or conversations. Reporting to our board and reflecting on the goals of our ministry with them are often the first line of defense against mission drift.

An effective board brings a variety of perspectives, mature faith and life experience to help focus our attention on our mission.

Share the Mission

Next Jethro advised Moses to select capable men who fear God and would not take bribes. We often find it difficult to share the ministry and focus on character. But that is what Jethro advised Moses to do.

We need to share ministry. We talk about this but often our heart is not in it. It is difficult to share ministry when we develop our identity and base our self-worth on the work we do. Many campus ministers have extensive training and years of ministry experience. We think we can do it better and faster. Then we find ourselves like Moses, burning the candle at both ends. Share the ministry, delegate the work to student leaders, board members and friends of the ministry. Ask yourself: what am I doing now that someone else can do? Then assign that task to a student leader, a volunteer, or a staff member.

As we think about sharing the work and delegating to others, we must look for people of character. Review your expectations for student leaders and board members. Are they written down and clearly understood? Too often we settle for people we like or are easy to work with. Jethro's list started with competence/skill, devotion to God and financial integrity. Every member of the board and ministry staff should demonstrate those traits. We should be developing students toward them as well.

Organize for the Mission

Organization. Planning. Hierarchy. Look again at the advice of Jethro: organize the capable men into "chiefs of thousands, of hundreds, of fifties, and of tens." Hierarchy and planning have to go with delegation and shared mission. When we delegate properly, we give responsibility and authority.

I know some of you are twitching as you read those words. You may be even thinking, "I got into ministry so I don't have to organize or plan and I definitely don't like hierarchy." But Jethro was onto something. Effective ministry requires a healthy organization that focuses on the mission.

I think our problem with hierarchy is two-fold. Many of the dysfunctional organizations and churches that we have experienced have lost their way with regard to mission. They no longer serve the mission God called them to serve. Second, dysfunctional organizations use people rather than serving them. You can spot these organizations because they are not life-giving. An effective board provides the leadership that serves an organization by focusing its attention on its mission and the people it serves.

Practices of an Effective Board

- **Intentional selection of board members**

Who are the members of your board? Do you have a plan or guidelines for the selection of new board members? Develop a plan involving two complementary descriptions of potential board members. The first set of expectations should be spiritual and attitudinal qualifications. Are they men and women of faith? Do they demonstrate evidence of a growing devotion to God? Are they men and women committed to church involvement and ministry? Are they advocates of the campus ministry with an attitude of support and encouragement? Board members should also represent your donors, supporters and alumni. If your ministry is funded heavily by churches, they should be represented accordingly.

The second set of descriptions should specify functional considerations for board members. How many alumni and non-alumni? Should you have pastors on your governing board? Are there women on your board? Do you have some important skill sets that come from law, education, finance, business, technology, insurance, etc?

A good selection plan for your board will also consider terms and length of service. We elect Directors to three-year terms staggered over three cycles. Directors can be elected to subsequent terms as long they are able to serve in an effective manner. Three or four-year terms allow for a conversation about continuing or concluding service in a timely manner. If a Director has to step off the board after one or two terms, that inhibits long-term thinking about the future of the ministry. We have found that it is good to have a balance of long-serving Directors and newer members. Two of our board members have served for over 30 years and they bring valued long-term perspective to our decision making.

- **Focus on Mission**

A critical responsibility of an effective board is to keep the ministry focused on its mission. Can everyone in the organization, starting with the board, state the mission? The board should be looking at the needed resources to support the mission and help develop a plan to build those resources. A good rule of thumb is that the governing board sets the mission. They also set the policy reflecting that mission. Staff and volunteers should be tasked with implementing the mission. That includes having sufficient authority to spend funds and develop programs to forward the mission of the organization.

The board should regularly discuss the mission of the organization with new board members.

Board meetings should focus on the mission. The board should regularly discuss the mission of the organization with new board members. The board should insist that the campus ministry staff and student leaders are committed to the mission. Reports to the board should reflect activity that moves the mission forward and identifies new opportunities to implement the mission. Financial reports should focus on responsible stewardship and adequate resources to implement the mission. Financial oversight should not be limited to keeping spending under control, but should also identify areas where increased funding is needed.

- **Develop an agenda for your meetings**

Effective boards recognize that board members need to manage their time well. Meetings should not waste time. An agenda is a plan for the board's time together. Increasingly, we are recognizing the importance of the spiritual components of scripture and prayer in our meetings. The agenda should list reports that will be presented, old business that is being tracked and new business that is being proposed.

One of the most important practices of our board is our annual retreat. We schedule a weekend that provides a longer look at some agenda items that cannot be covered well in 90 minutes on a Saturday. One practice we have built into our recent retreats is a time for our board members to get to know our student leaders through walks, prayer and meals. Our retreat is also the one time each year that our board and staff worship with each other. The priority on prayer and worship in these times helps build our culture of support and focus on our mission.

I also meet with our board chair a few weeks before the next scheduled meeting. We discuss the state of the ministry, review the previous board minutes, and discuss the agenda for the next meeting. There are often several months between some board meetings and I call the current chair frequently to keep them posted on what we are working on.

- **Consistent, Frequent Communication**

You cannot communicate too much with your governing board. An agenda with reports should be set prior to each meeting with sufficient time to review the documents. Minutes should be taken at the meeting and sent to the board after the meeting. Minutes should be a clear record of decisions made and actions taken during the meeting. They are the official, legal record of the ministry. Reminders of the meetings scheduled for the year should be sent via email and paper. Phone calls and email updates for board members in between meetings are a good practice. Send board members prayer requests in addition to business updates. Let them know their prayers are important.

You might read this and think it is a lot of work. However, if you want to have an effective, supportive board – you must communicate often and with substance. This is true of your donors and your family as well. Don't assume anyone already knows the information unless you enjoy last minute scurries to put out fires. Frequent, substantive communication builds trust and confidence. It is worth the extra work you put into it and it carries over to student ministry as well.

Look for board members who know how to listen.

- **Listen More, Speak Less**

Look for board members who know how to listen to each other, to staff and to student leaders. They should want to hear what everyone thinks. It is the best way to gather information, to make good decisions, and to be an effective advocate for the ministry. I find that if I have done the proper communication before the meeting, I can speak much less during the meeting. It gives time for other staff and student leaders to share what they are doing to serve the mission of the Campus House. This starts with me as the Campus Minister and our Chair. People enjoy meetings when they know they will be heard and what they care about is supported.

- **Shared Responsibility**

Set a staggered rotation of terms for board members. We have three-year terms with five members elected or re-elected each year with a total up to 15 serving on our board. We do not have automatic term retirement, members can continue to serve as long as they are effective. We use the expiration of the three-year term as a time to have a conversation about continued service and is an opportunity for a board member resign naturally if they feel the need to do so. It also provides an opportunity to have a conversation with a member who is not functioning up to expectations. A fellow board member should be involved in such conversations.

Rotate the board chair responsibilities. Our practice is for the chair to rotate after 1-2 years. Everyone is expected to serve as chair at some point in their tenure on the board. This prevents one member from dominating the board and provides for shared responsibility.

Organize your board into working teams. Identify the teams or committees your board needs to function well so the whole board can make good decisions. Examples of teams: finance, nominating, alumni, planning, facilities and an executive team. Your board may only require two or three functioning teams to help the full board function effectively.

We have found an executive committee to be very helpful. An executive committee can assist the board to respond immediately to a crisis or do extra work on a special project. For example, we used our executive committee to assist our staff in the process of purchasing property. The full board identified the financial limits of the purchase and authorized the executive committee to implement the details of the purchase instead of convening the full board every time a decision had to be made. An effective executive committee will require specific responsibilities and authority delegated by the full board.

Think Long Term

Developing an effective board culture is rooted in crucial, Biblical principles. Focus on mission, honor God and serve people. It takes work, time, prayer and planning. Short cuts may pay off today, but they are unfruitful in the long run. Think long term about your mission, yourself, and your family.

Mark Pike serves with the Christian Student Foundation at Ball State as senior campus minister where he has ministered for 33 years. He is married to Lynn and they have four children: Dylan, Olivia, Seth and Jaron. Mark and Lynn are members of Bethany Christian Church in Anderson, Indiana. Mark is a graduate of Emmanuel Christian Seminary (1990) and Great Lakes Christian College (1982).

Chapter 2

INFLUENCING A REGION

By Tim Hawkins

The word of the Lord spread through the whole region.
Acts 13:49

Maps tell us so much. They tell us where we have been and where we are going. Roads connect dots. Dots tell us where we are. Recently, I spent some time looking at a map that reflected where many denominational college ministries are located on university campuses throughout the USA. After looking closely, I noticed these organizations were sprawled throughout the Midwest, mostly in the "Bible Belt".

I was intrigued by four things:

- Campus ministries in New England (the six states of Maine, Vermont, New Hampshire, Massachusetts, Connecticut and Rhode Island).
- Campus ministries in California and Texas (the second and third largest states in the country, with massive college systems)
- Very few (at the time maybe 2-3) campus ministries west of Kansas/Oklahoma.
- Very few if any international campus ministries (not reflected on the map but an important observation).

Regions are Influenced through Strategic Partnerships and Locations

The Apostle Paul was never short a strategy. But, Paul was always open to altering his strategy through the influence of the Holy Spirit. The interplay between strategy and dynamic listening are essential to influencing a region. Paul chose strategic and influential cities within regions (Antioch of Pisidia, Paphos of Cyprus, Philippi, Athens, Corinth, Ephesus, Caesarea, Rome) as locations to create an influence and a stir that would reverberate through an entire region. Culturally significant regional centers that could sustain and launch regional movements and multiply the spreading of the good news were his focus.

Paul had a plan - he would go to the synagogues and share the message of God's fulfilling His promise to Israel, and then take the message to the Gentiles alerting them that God's plan had always included everyone.

Paul's audience would change, the local beliefs and cultural influences would change, and the questions, challenges and reception would change - but these two things remained relatively constant in Paul's strategy:

1. Go to influential cities.
2. Go from the synagogues to the streets.

This left the entire Roman world wide open.

The Apostle Paul wrote to the Romans,
It has always been my ambition to preach the gospel where Christ was not known, so that I would not be building on someone else's foundation. Rather, as it is written: "Those who were not told about him will see, and those who have not heard will understand." This is why I have often been hindered from coming to you" (Romans 15:22).

When applying his strategy and listening to the Holy Spirit, Paul had another value through which he would make decisions: whether or not a region had heard the gospel. This directly impacted choices he would make about where to go and where not to go.

Culturally significant regional centers that could sustain and launch regional movements and multiply the spreading of the good news were Paul's focus.

- Go to cultural centers.
- Go from the synagogues to the streets.
- Go to an area not yet reached.

Cultural Centers

Defining a cultural center depends somewhat on what you define as a region. And just as much how that city/region chooses you.

"During the night Paul had a vision of a man of Macedonia standing and begging him, 'Come over to Macedonia and help us.' After Paul had seen the vision, we got ready at once to leave for Macedonia, concluding that God had called us to preach the gospel to them." (Acts 16: 9-10)

This was not the norm for Paul. In fact, Paul wanted to go to Bithynia and Asia, but for some reason was not able to do so before Paul had this vision of Macedonia.

Sometimes a place chooses you.

It's probably nothing, I know, but when I got married over 24 years ago and 13 years before I would move to Boston, I wore a Boston Red Sox cap during the wedding ceremony! All of the groomsmen wore baseball caps, mine a Red Sox cap. (Don't worry, we took them off before the bridesmaids made their way down the aisle!) I was a baseball fan, but I'd never been to Boston, yet, the city already captivated me beyond baseball. So, when we began to bring college students out to work with church planters in New England, my heart was already predisposed to love the city. Maybe you have a place like that. I was drawn to the city. I can't fully rationally explain it. And I'm bound to over-spiritualize it.

When we first moved people would ask, "*Why Boston?*" And I'd respond, "*I love baseball, education and history...where else would be better than here?*" But there is more.

The summer before we were to move we spent some time with a Portuguese-speaking Brazilian church near Tufts University. We spent a lot of time on the roof of the library at Tufts University praying and seeking God about what He might be drawing us to.

One evening I had the opportunity to speak at the church. At the end of the evening, the pastor called people up who wanted to be anointed for God's work and blessing. This was striking against some of my more rational roots and making me slightly uncomfortable.

But, that night our daughter, who was seven at the time, went forward to be anointed for God's work and blessing, the only one in our family. She is now a Freshman at Tufts University sharing God's love by her actions and conversations, and studying from that same library from which we had been praying and listening to God.

Our Providence team leader hated Boston when he visited. To this day I think he is out of his mind. But, he visited Providence in Rhode Island, where there are six campuses and ten in the state the size of your thumb and very little college ministry work happening. The Lord drew his heart to Providence.

When a campus ministry at Georgia Tech began to have a vision for a college ministry that would impact Mexico City, they went to Monterey Tec and began talking with staff and students. One woman, in particular, wanted to share her testimony with them. In the words of Rick Harper, team leader:

Two years before our arrival on campus, she was downhearted about other world religions on campus and no Jesus. She told us one night, God woke her up and told her to claim her campus UAM for Jesus Christ. So, she got up in her bathrobe and slippers drove to her school and placed her hand on every building claiming it for Jesus Christ. She said since then no religion has set foot on this campus.

But then she stopped and said, "I knew you were coming to Mexico City. Four months ago, God told me in a dream that six gringos were coming down to start a movement that will change the world. I started counting us and there were five, and just then Rob came out from the bathroom. She had never seen him. So, I listened. And then over lunch in the middle of campus, a student came by and said, "I don't know who you are. But I was taking a nap and God woke me up and told me to come talk to you." By now we were blown away.

Identifying a cultural center depends on how you define the boundaries of a region. The University of Missouri-Columbia is the flagship campus in Missouri and serves as a cultural center for the state, but not necessarily the US. Boston is the cultural center of New England, but Providence serves that role in greater Rhode Island. Suffolk and UMASS are cultural centers for local residents of Boston, while

Harvard is a cultural center for world government and business. There are a lot of factors that go can go into choosing a location but, when it chooses you, you can be certain God is at work.

Synagogues to the Streets

Paul took time to go to the Synagogues, whether he went there first or last. If he was called to the Gentiles and to places where others had not yet shared the gospel, why bother at all with going to the Synagogue? After all, wouldn't others do that?

The synagogue was a cultural center for Jews away from the Temple in Jerusalem. This community center was always a gathering. It was also a place where "god-fearers" and "devout converts" (Acts 13), Gentiles who had come to believe in the God of Israel, would gather as part of the community. The synagogue was a bridge for Paul, from one world to the other, from Israel to the Gentiles and from the Gentiles to Israel.

Regional influence and impact are most effective when campus ministry serves as a bridge between the cultural influence of the church and the university

Regional influence and impact are most effective when campus ministry serves as a bridge between the cultural influence of the church and the university, a bridge that is open in both directions.

Sheila came to Jesus while she was a student at Wellesley College. She did not know a Christian growing up and her parents were culturally Catholic and Muslim (both non-practicing). Religion and faith were not a topic of conversation. After two friends died suddenly and tragically, she began seeking answers to those big questions about life. She did not do this through a college ministry or church, but began reading a Children's Bible she found on the shelf in her family library. When she reached the story of the resurrection of Jesus she began to sob and weep because, while she had heard of Jesus crucifixion, she had not heard the story of Jesus' resurrection.

She began attending a church after seeing advertisements on the subway. Soon after she was baptized. What Sheila craved in that season began with peers struggling with many of the same questions. Then she met older adults, those who had experience and answers. These were people not just defending vague ideas, but they arrived at answers from living faithful lives. She wanted to interact with those who reflected depth and maturity in life. People who listened and shared wisdom from walking a mile or two. Peers are where it started with Sheila. But her search was fulfilled by others she respected and admired, older folks who listened and cared.

The church became a bridge to a much bigger story that Sheila was finding herself a part of, and the college ministry was the bridge that was helping her understand and tell her story as part of the college community. The church is a cultural bridge to a much bigger story, but it is also a bridge for students to take that story with them to their campus.

As a ministry that stands alongside the church, campus ministry serves as an extension of the church. Campus ministry may be nonessential to reach the campus, but the church is indispensable.

Being affiliated with an independent and non-denominational movement like the Association of College Ministries or a church simply known as "Christian" can be an advantage in regions oversaturated by churches and denominational strife. Still, this can also be a disadvantage when establishing something in a new region.

Most of the colleges and universities in New England are private institutions, many with a Christian or religious heritage that predates the Restoration movement. "New" and "independent" are not trust building words with institutions embracing a long history with deep traditions.

One of the first questions we are asked on new campuses in New England is to identify our denomination. Identifying our ministry as "non-denominational" sends a message with a lot of baggage. What the university hears is, "Unaffiliated, without accountability, and dangerous."

Restoring Biblical Teaching and Experience

The letters of Paul are filled with conflict over Jewish and Gentile followers of Jesus! The authenticity of that tension makes the stories come to life with real-ness. I love how Paul calls them to love.

Reading First Corinthians backwards brings an entirely new perspective to life. See what happens when we start with 1 Corinthians 16:19-20, "*The churches in the province of Asia send you greetings. Aquila and Priscilla greet you warmly in the Lord, and so does the church that meets at their house. All the brothers and sisters here send you greetings. Greet one another with a holy kiss.*"

Remember we are following Jesus beyond ourselves

I often teach this by beginning every class having the students hug one another. "Before we get started in the meaning of the text today, let's start where Paul ends - I know holy kissing will seem strange, so we'll start with a holy hug,"

This puts everything into perspective as we then launch into reading the text of the Scripture lesson for the evening.

That is what I love about the church and about engaging rebellious, hormonally charged, experimental, nominally orthodox, barely Christian students in the church! It's also why I love for our rebellious, hormonally charged, experimental, nominally orthodox, barely Christian students to know narrow-minded, judgmental, know-it-alls. In the end...we have to set aside our differences and express our love for one another - a holy kiss.

An important attitude for campus ministers is to remember we are following Jesus beyond ourselves. We are part of a bigger story. And so is college ministry. We are part of a bigger story of God's church.

Tim Hawkins serves as Executive Director of Sojourn Collegiate Ministry located on college campuses in New England. Tim and his wife Stephanie help university students discover God's dream for their lives.

Chapter 3

ADVANCING ALUMNI RELATIONS

By Rob Schrumpf

A $350 million gift was recently pledged to Harvard University's School of Public Health. As the largest single donation in the university's long history, officials described how the contribution will help bolster research in several key areas. The donation came from the family of an alumni, T.H. Chan, a Hong Kong real estate developer, who earned his own master's degree from the public health school in 1979. The $350 million endowment was called, "transformational."

One of the many challenges of campus ministry is connected to the idea of alumni relations. How do we create relationships with the students who walk in our doors for just a handful of months or years; and then how do we maintain and advance these relationships once these students have moved on from our campuses to face the jobs and relationships and mortgages of adulthood in the "real world?" How do we invite them to own the vision? How do we encourage them to continue to partner with us in prayer, disciple-making, and mission?

First Steps: Alumni relations begin when freshmen first walk through the door

There are several ways throughout the year that we strive to connect our students with the bigger storyline of the ministry. While being careful not to diminish the current students' present campus ministry, we try to help them understand that they are a part of something that has been around for 50 years—a ministry that started with just six students who wanted to see the Gospel take root on the campus. We share with them the framework of how we exist and the fact that there are literally thousands of alums who have worshipped in the same space, alums who continue to pray for and support this ministry so that every generation of students can experience a transformed life in Christ.

Connections and Mentorship

We regularly have alums come speak to our present students at our worship gatherings or retreats, or join a mission trip or event. Occasionally an alumnus will mentor or disciple a student or lead a group.

Sending Base

As part of our weekly worship service, we take up an offering, a significant portion of which supports recent grads who are doing vocational ministry or missions. This is a way to teach the theology of giving, generosity, and God's economy. However, it also serves as yet another way to connect alums and their stories to our present students, and it creates a reciprocating appreciation, as well.

How best do we tell the story?

Senior Sunday

As we prayerfully commission and send new graduates out the door, we encourage their continuation of personal discipleship, church involvement, and ongoing connectedness to Campus House. We reiterate how Campus House is financially supported and ask them to consider becoming an ongoing partner in the ministry.

Week of Thanks

Each fall and spring, our students and staff participate in a "Week of Thanks" where they make phone calls and write notes of gratitude to supporters (many of whom are alums), simply thanking them and sharing a bit of their own story and Campus House experience. This bi-annual event is a huge encouragement to both present students and alums.

Entry Point of Support

We start by asking them to pledge to support the incoming freshman all the way through their senior year by praying for and donating to Campus House over the next four years.

Next Steps: The Ongoingness of Alumni Relations is Rooted in Story

Storytelling is relational glue: a framework for building connections, casting vision, and deepening ownership. Storytelling is an art form that communicates far more than the transfer of information, stats, and spreadsheets. When current students share their experiences with alumni, these stories connect with the heart. These stories contextualize the memories of alums within the present realities of the 18 to 22 year-olds who sit where they once sat.

So the question: How best do we tell the story?

When it comes to the use of technology in maintaining and growing alumni relations, the question is not whether we should use technology (we should); but rather, "How do we use technology most effectively to both tell the overall story of the ministry and target specific groups of alums?" Designating certain platforms for specific purposes is a starting point. Asking, "What is the function of our website? How and why do we use social media? Who exactly are we trying to reach, and how could we do this more effectively?

Newsletters

We publish a newsletter five or six times a year that highlights a specific area of ministry, conveys staff and student stories, showcases photos from recent events and mission trips, and furnishes financial updates and existing needs—in both a printed and digital version.

Social Media

We use social media to post upcoming events and sermon series and to tell stories through photos, but to also launch campaigns specified to alums and highlight moments from Campus House's history.

Website

Our website functions as a connecting place for present and potential students, but also as a reconnecting piece for alums, offering podcasts, a link to the newsletter, and (coming soon) the alumni portal.

Alumni Portal

One of our new projects is an online alumni portal and map where alums of the ministry can build a profile, post a pin of where they are in the world, and elect to share part of their ongoing story in the Kingdom. The purpose of the map is to help us reconnect with alums we've lost track of, provide a platform to connect alums with each other, collect stories of what God is continuing to do in their lives, compile relevant information for better communication, and to give our recent graduates a connection with alums in the place they are moving— potentially affording us a new wealth of relationships and stories.

Plan and Assess

Organizing a 12-24 month plan for the use of social media, website, campaigns and newsletters is important. Develop a philosophy and methodology for communicating the story (and collecting the ongoing stories) of your alums. Incorporate ways to regularly assess the processes of communication and the depth of alumni connection through surveys and feedback.

Tools for the Trade

When it comes to tracking alumni information, there is a wide range of software systems, ranging from a good introductory system like Aplos (www.aplos.com) that starts at $25/month to a complete fundraising cloud-based software like Raiser's Edge which can cost $5000 to $10,000 a year. (You can review a list of options at: http://www.capterra.com/fundraising-software/)

What is a reasonable allotment of time and resources to pour into alumni relations?

Another foundational question is, "What is a reasonable allotment of time and resources to pour into alumni relations?" With this in mind, each ministry needs to take the time to discover which system is best for their context and budget. For us, customization of donor websites and e-newsletters, ease of batch processing, and the ability to create and query any donor field were key in our software decision; but for others, the primary selling points might be customer support and financial software integration.

At the very least, every ministry must be able to:

- Accurately update contact information and record the activities in which alumni were involved as students.
- Record gifts and be able to issue tax-deductible receipts.
- Have the ability to create donation pages and e-communications.

Face to Face

The most effective way to maintain and advance alumni relations is through face to face, knee to knee conversations and ongoing discipleship. Beyond one-on-one meetings with alums, we utilize our Annual Thank You Dinner, various reunions, and have four alumni-related initiatives each year that allow us to reconnect personally, share ministry updates and prayer requests, and to catch up with what is going on in their lives and faith journeys. While admitting that there are obvious limitations to sustaining relationships with alums and that our priority of time and energy spent should (most days) be on our present students, what a privilege it is to have ongoing opportunities to pastor and counsel, to offer resources and church connections, to officiate their weddings, to meet their babies, and then 18 years later, to meet their now-college-freshman

Reasons for Donating:

Recent research highlights several factors that are involved in Alumni partnerships with schools and institutions. First, there is **an emotional connection.** Drivers for donating are emotional. Nearly half of donors (49 percent) say they feel "very close" to their organization, compared to just 16 percent of non-donors. They feel a deep connection and feel a sense of community. Additionally, nearly eighty percent of donors say they have personally benefitted from their connection with the group.

Reasons for Not Donating:

Some alumni are not able to partner with the campus ministry financially and here are the primary reasons why:

- Not Within Budget. Many say they cannot currently donate because they "can't afford to" donate to their alma mater.
- Worthier Causes. Another segment of alumni say there are worthier causes and organizations to give to.
- Lack of Effective Communications. Forty-seven percent of non-donor respondents say they never received any communication via social media from their school, and 31 percent do not receive invitations to alumni events and activities. Forty-four percent of non-donors say they receive no information on current school programs
- Yearning for Alumni Services. Thirteen percent of non-donors believe their college or university offers no alumni services at all.

Surprisingly, forty-seven percent of non-donors claim they are interested in getting more involved in some capacity with their college or university.

Campus ministry is an outpost of the Kingdom.

"Alumni want to feel emotionally connected with their alma maters, and it's crucial that colleges and universities increase their communications in an effective way in order to grow engagement – and ultimately fundraise – from their alumni base," Ellison said. *"The results of the survey have shown us that higher education*

institutions need to make better connections with their alumni. Utilizing today's innovative tools in the right way, like digital and social media platforms, will enable schools to make more meaningful connections with their alumni."

The Revolving Door of Campus Ministry

Campus Ministry is an outpost of the Kingdom, commissioning and launching alums into every part of the globe, workforce, and society. There is a revolving door motif where the individual comes in off the street and is "in the lobby" for a few years until they head back out into the real world. The data would show that those years are some of the most significant in their life. Many, if not most, students who come through the collective doors of our ministries have a transformational encounter with the grace of Jesus, experience authentic community, and have a radical shift in life purpose and direction. Eventually, they transition out through the same revolving door; but they are forever changed and eternally grateful for a place and a group of people who loved them well and deepened their walk with Christ. The God-stories of these alums are ongoing, as are the relationships that were forged inside the walls of our campus ministries, and spilled out into the streets of our campuses and cities.

May God perpetuate the process and build His Kingdom and may He leverage generation after generation of campus ministry alumni along the way.

Rob Schrumpf is Lead Pastor at Purdue Christian Campus House, a campus church at Purdue University in West Lafayette, Indiana. A graduate of Johnson University, he has served at Campus House since 1988 in a mixture of roles that include teaching, pastoral counseling, discipleship, leadership development, and cultural engagement. Rob is married to Lea, who is an incredible part of the Campus House staff team, and they have three adult children and a son-in-law who are all pretty amazing.

Chapter 4

IN PURSUIT OF PROFESSIONALISM

By Cindy Swinney

"When I think of professionalism I think of a nice tie and dress shoes, not using bad words, being formal in your speech, but it means more than that. It has more complex layers than that...."

When the University of California-Irvine Career Center interviewer ventured out onto the campus video camera in hand, this was one student's response when asked "What is professionalism?" The 2015 YouTube video[1] continues with opinions from twelve students with twelve quite different answers. A sampling of their responses are:

- Knowing what your goal is, going for it, and knowing how to work with different personalities, but still stand your ground in what you are trying to achieve.
- Having your clothes pressed, having your hair combed, having your makeup applied, having your shoes match. All these things reflect on you when you enter a meeting or an interview. They set the tone for how you conduct yourself after that.
- Being engaged in whatever you are doing currently. If you are in a meeting actively taking notes, you aren't

[1] https://www.youtube.com/watch?v=K3L-_Nbki0Q (accessed May 27, 2016).

scanning Facebook or checking other email. Making sure you are focused, engaged in the conversation…

- Devotion to your profession and in yourself as a person. Really, how you show your best strengths.
- For me personally, things like formality or maybe traditional definitions like dress and things like that don't really matter as much. It is about the work people are doing, what they are able to produce, that they can be proud of their work at the end of the day.
- Professionalism is to me being able to hold yourself in a manner presentable to the professional world aside from what you do in your life outside your profession. Being professional is being able to set that apart and carry yourself in a way that demands respect and shows that you are serious about what you do.

So many diverse responses to a seemingly simple question! It's about the individual. It's about the organization. It's about what you do. It's about your attitude. It's about your goals. All the answers are correct! There is so much truth in the response that there are many complex layers of professionalism. This book will break down professionalism into two areas: Face-to-face, day-to-day interactions between the campus minister and real people, and secondly, "Techno-Professionalism," or development of professionalism when immersed in the world of technology and its challenges.

For a down-to-earth definition, today's culture clicks to the popular, easily accessible sources of what has replaced the fat, red Webster's Dictionary. Check these out:

- The practice of a member of a profession or any person who earns their living from a specified activity; does mainly mental work as opposed to engaging in physical work *(Wikipedia)*[2]

- Professionalism is not defined by the way a person is dressed, however, the profession should define how the person dresses…. Professionalism includes but is not limited to accountability, integrity, compassion, and excellence. *(Yahoo Answers)*
- In the business world, professionalism means holding oneself to a higher standard. Including, but not limited to; 1) Adhering to certain codes of ethics, appearance, attitude, etcetera; 2) Going above and beyond expectations; 3) Maintaining composure and decorum; 4) Striving to do the job right the first time; 5) Being capable of wisely evaluating whether to be self-reliant or to outsource assistance….. (*Answers.com)*[3]

Students have opinions while the Internet spouts multiple definitions, so where can campus ministers gain clear direction about professionalism and determine its importance in campus ministry? These two chapters will examine not a definition, but the learned conduct that radiates professionalism.

Susie Kay, author of Professionalism: The ABC for Success, writes: *"Professionalism is not just for those who work in the traditional professions. It is for you and me and all of our colleagues and friends, whether we are students, doctors, architects, work in a factory, a coffee shop, an office*

[2] *"What Does Professionalism Mean to You?"*, response from PINK, https://answers.yahoo.com/question/index?qid=20070218205706AAAsSJu (accessed May 27, 2016).

[3] *"What is Professionalism?"* response by Rocky B, http://www.answers.com/Q/Professionalism_means_what (accessed May 27, 2016).

or anywhere else that we come in contact with others." It is no wonder that are so many ideas and opinions what this undefinable behavior!

Kay summarizes, *"Some say that those who exude professionalism have a 'certain something,' hard to put your finger on but you know it when you see it."* Yes, it is in manners, the way one dresses and speaks, and certainly on how well one does his job. But in addition, professionalism reflects the individual's obvious standards of excellence and his desire to earn and maintain respect. This applies not just in the workplace, but within the family, social circle, at church, at sporting events, even in the grocery store. It's about the total package – what we do and what we are. Everything.

Really? Professionalism in Ministry?

Why not? Doctors, lawyers, dentists, and accountants have all achieved a high level of knowledge and skill, and are in fields where they have earned the label of "professional." A highly educated, five-star rated, world-renown physician at the Mayo Clinic can be a great surgeon and never have to smile. Bedside manner is certainly a plus, but knowing the best doctor in his field is holding the scalpel during the patient's surgery trumps his eating Cheerios for breakfast.

Ministers also offer a service of tremendous value to individuals from all walks of life. These professionals have also achieved degrees, knowledge, and skill yet would never be considered successful without a positive attitude and a warm smile – key components to professional conduct. Dale Atkins in a TEDxYouth talk shared his thoughts to a group of young people.

"(Professionalism) is an odd word, not just a label or title. Attitudes, behaviors, actions. Combine these three to

get a profound implication. Attitudes drive behaviors, which in turn drive actions. Actions reinforce attitudes ... the process is not an event – it is a journey."[4]

Atkins' framework to being a professional in the secular business world fits surprisingly well in ministry:

- Knowing. Learn all you can and as much as you can. It is more than just awareness. You need to understand and take that knowledge and apply it.
- Doing. Develop skills to realize there are many options and solutions to solving problems.
- Helping. Being there for people. Making a difference in people's lives
- Learning. Commit to being a lifelong learner. Yesterday's knowledge and skills aren't always good enough to solve tomorrow's problems.

Ministry takes knowledge and wisdom. Isn't Atkins saying from a secular standpoint what the Bible teaches to students of God's Word? *Knowledge* comes from reading, personal experiences, and even relationships – all of a worldly nature. But even memorizing the Bible and having all that knowledge does not insure one has wisdom. *Wisdom* is taking the knowledge in God's Word and applying it to everyday life.

Knowing, doing, helping, learning. Each is important to the secular professional, but even more so to Christian leaders serving the Lord on and off-campus.

---

[4] Atkins, Dale. (May 4, 2013). Being A Professional: Dale Atkins at TEDxYouth@EHS [Video file]. Retrieved from https://www.youtube.com/watch?v=sLv7sdGJWPI

Why is professionalism important?

Professionalism is a choice made every day. It provides an opportunity for one to think, behave and act in a way that will make him stand out from the crowd. Imagine three doors available to open at the beginning of each day. The first door is labeled "Minimal." The second says "Mediocre" and the third door says "Excellence." Which is the best choice?

- **Minimal.** Do the minimum. Be nice. Make the least effort possible to keep a job. Warning: Most campus ministries have one staff with no day to day supervision. This is by far the easiest and most tempting choice. The unspoken attitude is, "Who will know if I play golf with my buddy instead of putting effort into this week's teaching or meeting with students?" James 4:17 says, "So whoever knows the right thing to do and fails to do it, for him it is sin." Satan no doubt smiles on those who choose this door!
- **Mediocre**. The person who chooses to open this door plans to do enough to be average. He will throw out some encouragement or compassion as it is convenient and comfortable, and work in a way that is visible to others, though not at a level to which he is capable and gifted. Romans 12:11 reads: *"Do not be slothful in zeal, be fervent in spirit, serve the Lord."* God does not call believers to be average. Author Shannon Alder is quoted as saying, *"If you were born with the ability to change someone's perspective or emotions, never waste that*

God has called His children to live a life of excellence so each one can reflect His glory and excellence

gift. It is one of the most powerful gifts God can give—the ability to influence."

- **Excellence**. Choosing to walk through this door means making a commitment to strive for excellence. It does not mean imposing demands for perfection at every step, but taking what one has and doing the very best with it.

Consider II Peter 1:3 (ESV). *"His divine power has granted to us all things that pertain to life and godliness, through the knowledge of him who called us to his own glory and excellence."*

> *His divine power has granted to us all things.*

God has called His children to live a life of excellence so each one can reflect His own glory and excellence. Most professions demand excellence in the quality of work, appearance, and even demeanor, but the decision to answer God's call to ministry means accepting that the standard of excellence is much higher in this field. Where many can stow their 'professional hat' when they leave the office, a minister wears it 24/7. Ministers indeed live in a fishbowl:

- At the workplace. Whether in a church, parachurch, walking on the college campus, or even in a secular job, a minister's choices are noticed – and judged – through an Ultra HD lens. How does this person interact with students? Interns and support staff? Board members? Prayer and financial supporters such as church leaders and individuals? College staff including not just administrators but faculty and custodians?

- At home. Going the extra mile to maintain healthy relationships with a spouse and children.
- At play. An active social life means spending time with family, friends, peers, and students, having fun, laughing and enjoying life in a way that reflects Christian values. Believers AND non-believers are watching each move of the person who professes Christian faith, especially ministers. Fair? No, but it is reality in today's culture just as it was when Jesus walked near the Pharisees and Sadducees.

What does a life lived with excellence look like? Every day, decide to demonstrate an attitude that inspires trust and confidence from all with whom one interacts. Attitude drives behavior, and behavior communicates values and character.

Values. Character. Those are some meaty words that begin to bring into focus the importance of professionalism. When someone asks "What's that campus minister like?" everyone wants to hear that he has values and character, and then adjectives thrown in like trustworthy, competent, considerate, empathetic, courteous, dependable, cooperative, intelligent, committed, approachable, supportive, responsible, integrity, and perseverance.

These words can all go into the "total package" describing someone sporting professionalism, but come on! Is it even possible for one person – one student, one campus minister, one anything – to evolve into Mr. Perfect Professional?

Unlikely. But in the strife for excellence, the bar is set and must remain very high. Paul wrote to Timothy what is expected of a Christian leader:

"Don't let anyone look down on you because you are young, but set an example for the believers in speech, in conduct, in love, in faith and in purity. Until I come, devote yourself to the public reading of Scripture, to preaching and to teaching. Do not neglect your gift, which was given you through prophecy when the body of elders laid their hands on you. Be diligent in these matters; give yourself wholly to them, so that everyone may see your progress. Watch your life and doctrine closely. Persevere in them, because if you do, you will save both yourself and your hearers." (1 Timothy 4:12-16)

Paul's list is narrowed down to a leader's conduct, speech, love, faith, and purity. For this chapter, the list will be narrowed down and simplified even further. Professionalism in campus ministry boils down to the "ABCs" of life: Attitude, Behavior, Communication.

Attitude

Charles Swindoll teaches that in spite of all the things in life that cannot be changed, there is one thing over which there is total control.

> *"The longer I live, the more I realize the impact attitude has on life.... It is more important than the past, than education, than money, than circumstances, than failures, than successes, than what other people think or say or do. It is more important than appearance, giftedness or skill. It will make or break a company...a church...a home. The remarkable thing is we have a choice every day regarding the attitude we will embrace for the day. We cannot change our past. We cannot change the fact that people will act in a certain way. We cannot change the inevitable. The only thing we can do is*

play on the one string we have, and that is our attitude. I am convinced that life is 10% what happens to me and 90% how I react to it. And so it is with you. We are in charge of our attitudes."[5]

What does a positive attitude look like? Whether a campus minister is playing bocce ball with students, spending an evening with family, meeting with the Board of Directors, or participating in a retreat with peers, his demeanor is the same. Time Management Ninja came up with a list of 21 Ways to Define a Positive Attitude. Here is a sampling of the list:

- Enjoying the unexpected, even when it's not what you wanted originally.
- Motivating those around you with a positive word.
- Using the power of a smile to reverse the tone of a situation.
- Being friendly to those you don't know.
- Being a source of energy that lifts those around you.
- Having a good time even when you are losing.
- Having a positive future vision, no matter how bad your current circumstances.
- Smiling.
- Paying a compliment, even to a total stranger.
- Not letting other people's negativity bring you down.

[5] Swindoll, Charles R. "The Poem: Attitude," Retrieved from http://thelittlerebellion.com/index.php/2012/11/new-club-on-campus-embraces-bodies-and-beauty/bbp-poem-2/.

Be someone who others want to be with because you lift their energy, attitude, and spirit. Be someone who you would want to be around. Choose to have a positive attitude.[6]

Behavior

It follows naturally that one who chooses to have a positive attitude will make excellent choices in his behavior, which is simply how one conducts himself in daily activities. It is easy to spot someone who is *misbehaving* because he is not acting properly, displaying a rebellious or self-centered attitude, or reacting in a way that draws negative attention. Think "tired-toddler-in-grocery-store-with-exhausted-mother" and the picture quickly comes into view.

If misbehavior is acting *improperly,* then good behavior is acting *properly*. What does this look like for a campus minister? Simply put, it is acting in a manner that draws positive attention, admiration, and respect. This applies at home, at the workplace, in social circles and certainly in all aspects of ministry work. Proper behavior for a campus minister includes appropriate appearance, good manners, politeness, respectable communication skills.... Picture the "total package" referred to earlier.

Etiquette is a rather old word for "manners," and parallels – even intersects with – today's word "professionalism." Etiquette changes just as culture changes. Many of the old traditions of Emily Post regarding typical manners and behaviors have shifted, while others stand firm. According to a poll on American manners by the Associated

[6] Jarrow, Craig. February 24, 2012. "21 Ways to Define a Positive Attitude." Retrieved from https://timemanagementninja.com/2012/02/21-ways-to-define-a-positive-attitude/

Press-Ipsos[7], 69% of those polled think people are more rude than 20 or 30 years ago. The responses on the possible causes of rudeness and where a great or fair deal of blame should be placed were:

- 69% said "celebrities, athletes and public figures are rude and poor role models"
- 93% felt parents not teaching good manners to their children
- 73% say it is TV shows and movies that show rude behavior

Another question asked "Do you encounter this situation frequently, occasionally, rarely, or never? The percentages who answered "frequently" were:

- People using their cell phones in a loud or annoying manner in public: 55%
- People using rude or offensive language in public: 48%
- Drivers who are aggressive and reckless on the road: 55%
- Children behaving rudely in public: 44%

Behavior is a reflection of one's attitude. Road rage – a behavior – is merely a person's attitude of "This road is MINE. I am more important. Don't get in MY way." Pride shows up in the strangest places!

Proverbs 11:2 reminds believers *"when pride comes, then comes disgrace, but with humility comes wisdom."* Campus

---

[7] USA Today and Associated Press. October 14, 2005. "American Manners Poll," Retrieved from < http://usatoday30.usatoday.com/news/nation/2005-10-14-rudeness-poll-method_x.htm>

ministers who conduct themselves in a professional manner need to know and practice good manners.

Plain, Common Sense Manners

In the article "Etiquette for Twentysomethings," Relevant Magazine came up with a list of rules that goes beyond knowing how to shake hands and chew with the mouth closed. June Hines Moore writes, *"Together (these rules) keep us from embarrassing ourselves or someone else. The rules give us confidence and the manners tell us when to break or ignore a rule if the other person would be made uncomfortable."* Moore says there are some specific rules twentysomethings tend to break or ignore:

> *Do your best to return phone calls within 24 hours.*

- Not responding to an R.S.V.P. (on time or at all) or not writing thank you notes.
- Not identifying themselves when making a phone call.
- Not returning phone calls within 24 hours.
- Wearing caps in restaurants or using toothpicks in public.
- Bringing a friend to a party you are invited to when the invitation doesn't say "and guest" or without checking with the hostess first.
- Offering a chair to someone older on public transportation.
- Holding a door open for someone older or for any woman.
- Standing back and to the side of an elevator door until all have exited before attempting to get in.

- Saying "You're welcome!" rather than "No problem." It requires no extra effort.
- Failing to introduce people or claiming to forget someone's name (an effort should be made even if we must admit we can't remember)
- Being on time. Plan ahead and always leave a bit of extra room in every daily schedule. Few things draw more negative attention than someone entering a meeting late.[8]

Many things have not changed since the days of Emily Post, an American author famous for writing about etiquette. She is quoted as saying, *"Manners are a sensitive awareness of the feelings of others. If you have that awareness, you have good manners, no matter what fork you use."*[9]

Behavior - Appearance

Learning and practicing good etiquette is a key component of professionalism, but acting the part isn't enough. Whether it is a weekend ministry during college years, or full-time ministry following graduation, a minister is expected to look professional.

What constitutes appropriate attire for ministry? In 2016, feisty discussions run rampant on social media on whether or not yoga pants are okay in the workplace. Just as feisty are the whispered conversations between some senior citizens when their minister opts to preach in blue jeans.

---

[8] Hines, Julia. "Etiquette for Twentysomethings." Relevant Magazine. Retrieved from http://www.relevantmagazine.com/life/relationship/features/1801-etiquette-for-twentysomethings#FuH6YkiHfbHyssxv.99 October 2003.

[9] Post, Emily. Inspirational Quotes about Life. Retrieved from http://www.quotes-inspirational.com/by/emily-post/ Date written unknown.

Professional attire does not mean touting a spiffy suit with a white shirt though in some fields that is appropriate. It does not mean shelling out megabucks for the latest fashions at the trendy boutique of the month. It is quite simply wearing clothes that fit the occasion. What a campus minister wears when invited to a church to talk about thc campus ministry's work should be a quite different look from what he wears to hang out on a weeknight with college students. Think of the choices available and where each might be appropriate:

- Casual – jeans or shorts, flip-flops, baseball cap, t-shirt. This look may be fine for hanging out on campus or even in a coffee meeting near campus with a student. For females in ministry, casual dress does not include immodest clothes with low-cut necklines, short shorts or skin-tight anything. Ragged or dirty clothes reflect laziness anywhere but activities like tackle football where dirt is involved.
- Business Casual – khakis or Dockers®, shirt with a collar (full front buttons or three button golf-type shirt), closed toed shoes with socks. For females, it is full-length slacks or below the knee skirt with a modest sweater, blouse, or jacket. Many campus ministers choose to dress business casual when doing large group teaching or meeting with supporters or board members. When attending a conference like ICOM plan to dress business casual for the entire stay. This is the appropriate attire for working at a ministry exhibit booth, attending workshops and lunches, main sessions, and all meetings.
- Business Dress – nice pants, collared shirt (white, colored, or small pattern/pinstriped), sport coat with or without tie, closed toed shoes with matching socks.

For females, business dress is a below-the-knee skirt or dress, modest top perhaps with a coordinating jacket, dressy shoes and, yes, nylons – particularly when meeting with middle-aged or older individuals. This is an appropriate way to dress when preaching in a church or presenting ministry work to a Missions Team or potential financial supporters.

- Formal – suit, collared shirt, coordinating necktie for men, below the knee dress or skirt with modest top for women. Professional attire for a campus minister at a wedding, a funeral, and most formal banquets.

Yikes! The dollar signs are spinning! How can someone on a campus minister's salary afford such a wardrobe? Fortunately, there are many sources for good quality, fashionable clothing in most cities.

- Don't frown at the thought of Salvation Army and Goodwill; both offer tons of choices in every possible size of any clothing piece just listed. Two or three sets of business casual clothes are commonly available for $10-$15 each and 30 minutes to shop.
- Craig's List generally has several choices of suits and sport coats as well as all other kinds of clothes, though it might take a few tries to find something in the right size.
- Put on a suit of armor and hit the department stores the week after Christmas. Even into January, a savvy shopper with a fistful of newspaper coupons and a little time can buy a nice supply of brand new clothes for under $100!
- Many churches both large and small host a monthly or periodic Clothing Exchange or Giveaway. Donors give nice clothes in hopes they will be enjoyed by

someone with minimal funds for a wardrobe. By making a few phone calls, find and keep track of these events and participate as often as possible.

- Garage sales are fun and can reap huge savings for good quality clothing for any occasion. Consider it entertainment instead of shopping and it's a hoot!

In her article "Dress with Confidence – How Dressing Affects Your Attitude and Confidence," Sheila Dicks writes: *"Dressing with confidence is more than wearing the latest fashion trend, it's about feeling good about what you're wearing, looking poised and feeling self-assured in all situations."* Yes, how one dresses can affect attitude and self-confidence.[10]

If a campus minister feels more confident by dressing appropriately, others will tend to listen more attentively to what is being said. Confidence breeds confidence. Imagine sitting in an airplane seat awaiting takeoff and the pilot boards wearing baggy sweatpants and dirty tennis shoes. The pilot may feel confident, but the impression of his expertise from everyone else on the plane takes a quick, sharp nosedive.

For those campus ministers still doubting the value of appropriate dress, consider the study done at Northwestern University described in Rebecca Silveria's article "Dress Well, Test Well." The objective was to determine the effect of clothing on psychological process and performance. A great point they made is the influence of not only the actual appearance of the appropriate clothes but the symbolic meaning that comes along with them. For example, a suit and

[10] Dicks, Sheila. "Dress With Confidence – How Dressing Affects Your Attitude and Confidence." Retrieved from http://www.selfgrowth.com/articles/Dress_with_Confidence_How_Dressing_Affects_Your_Attitude_and_Confidence.html, October 2006.

tie is known by all to be professional, formal, official and maybe even convey intelligence, dedication and expertise.[11]

This thinking isn't new, and in fact goes back to the horse and buggy days. Lady Duff-Gordon (1863-1935) is quoted as saying, *"Put even the plainest woman into a beautiful dress and unconsciously she will try to live up to it."*[12]

A campus minister needn't – and shouldn't – feel the need to sport a suit or a fancy dress to be successful and earn respect in every day work. He should, however, develop a habit of considering the occasion and the audience of those with whom he interacts on any given day, then make a choice to dress appropriately.

First impressions do count.

An accounting professor at the University of Nebraska knows from firsthand experience that dressing well can improve test scores, and has a requirement for her students to dress business casual on exam days. It did, however, comes as a surprise on the first exam day when there was an obvious differing opinion on the meaning of business casual. Many of the females in her class had interpreted this attire to mean necklines go down and hems go up. This met the current fashion trend for "dressing up" but was certainly not appropriate in a professional or academic setting.

---

[11] Silveria, Rebecca. "Dress Well, Test Well." Retrieved from http://www.personal.psu.edu/afr3/blogs/siowfa13/2013/10/dress-well-test-well.html, October 2013

[12] Duff-Gordon Lucy Lady. AZ Quotes Retrieved from http://www.azquotes.com/author/46836-Lucy_Lady_Duff_Gordon Date written unknown.

Any female campus minister wants to earn respect and should not draw unnecessary attention to her looks by wearing immodest though fashionable clothing.

Clancy Cross goes into further detail about the aspects of dressing as a matter of respect in his article "The ABC's of Professionalism: Dress Up." He writes, "Respect yourself with the way you dress and your overall attitude of professionalism will rise to a new level. Dressing with respect includes good hygiene. At the risk of stating the obvious, here is my list of keywords: soap, razor, deodorant, toothpaste, toothbrush, cologne, comb and nail clippers. Mom was right when she told you to wash behind the ears, comb your hair, brush your teeth and trim your nails. In case Mom's not around to check up on you, here's a tip. If you draw blood when shaking hands, it's time to trim your nails."

Cross goes on to say, "For women, there is a difference between attractive and sexy. Displaying cleavage, thighs, and/or a bare midriff is unprofessional for *most* careers (if you get my point.)"[13]

Professional, appropriate appearance is not limited to just the right clothing but expands on to include "accessories." If a campus minister chooses to look nontraditional with body piercings, excessive and gaudy tattoos, and outrageous hairstyles and facial hair, expect to work twice as hard to earn respect from nearly all those whom you meet in your ministry work. An attempt to be trendy or fashionable on campus might well be a turnoff to church leaders, financial supporters, board members, university administrators, and even prayer partners. First impressions DO count.

[13] Cross, Clancy. "The ABCs of Professionalism: Dress Up." Retrieved from https://clancycross.com/2008/08/25/dress-up, August 2008.

Professional appearance is a choice, according to Cross. *"You might be thinking, 'Well, this really isn't who I am. I'm not* a *'suit and tie kinda person.'"* Next, you might be thinking this is going to be hard. What's the alternative?

Think about which path to success is most difficult. The first way is to make the necessary changes in yourself to project a professional image. The second way is to make no personal changes and devote your energies to convince everyone that you are a professional in spite of your unprofessional appearance. In other words, change thousands of opinions. The third option is to choose a profession which demands less in the way of appearance."[14]

When striving for excellence, remember Paul's words in 1 Corinthians 6:19-20 (ESV):

"Or do you not know that your body is a temple of the Holy Spirit within you, whom you have from God? You are not your own, for you were bought with a price. So glorify God in your body."

Communication

It bears repeating. Attitude determines behavior. An important part of any campus minister's behavior is how well he communicates with others. This could be a phone conversation, an email, a comment on social media, an internet blog, a website article, a letter, and last but certainly not least, face to face conversations. What is professional behavior when it comes to communications with others?

---

[14] Cross, Clancy. "The ABCs of Professionalism: Dress Up." Retrieved from https://clancycross.com/2008/08/25/dress-up, August 2008.

Conversation and Listening

"The character of a man is known from his conversations." — Menander (342 BC – 292 BC) Who would think that even before the birth of Jesus people were talking about the art and effect of good conversation? In his article "Constructive Conversation," Clancy Cross states that professional conversation is first and foremost about being a good listener. Becoming so is nothing more than learning to care more about what the other person is saying than what you want to say.

- **Listen like you care** — it shows respect. It has the added advantages of keeping you more alert and helping you to remember more.
- **Listen like you'll be tested**. Unless it's a business conversation this doesn't mean taking notes. Just try to remember the key points. This technique will reinforce your attitude toward listening.
- **Listen as if there's a hidden gem** in what the talker is saying that you can't afford to miss. Yes, this applies even when he rambles on with no apparent end in sight.
- **Listen with your eyes.** When listening (and speaking), look at the person's face, not out the window, at your cell phone or at the television.[18]

Few can describe the importance of listening better than Maya Angelou, an American author, poet, and civil rights activist in the late 1990s: *"People may not remember what you did or said, but they will remember how you made them feel."*[15]

---

[15] Cuddy, Amy. "Your Body Language Shapes Who You Are." TEDtalks, Retrieved from http://www.ted.com/talks/amy_cuddy_your_body_language_shapes_who_you_are, June 2012.

Non-Verbal Conversation

One of the most listened to TED Talks is "Your Body Language Shapes Who You Are" by Amy Cuddy. As a social psychologist, she knows *"body language governs not only how others see us, but how we see ourselves. 'Power posing' -- standing in a posture of confidence, even when we don't feel confident -- can affect testosterone and cortisol levels in the brain, and might even have an impact on our chances for success."*

Bodies change minds, minds change behavior, and behavior changes outcomes. Feels fake? Fake it till you make it. Fake it till you become it.

A campus minister can establish a presence with positive body language – that "certain something that hard to put your finger on but you know it when you see it." A few tweaks to improve body language can reflect passion, enthusiasm, authenticity, and confidence. Cuddy concludes by encouraging listeners to "bring your best self to every conversation."[20]

People may not remember what you did or said, but they will remember how you made them feel

The University of Georgia Career Center surveyed students and employers to find varying opinions about non-verbal behavior. They found 56% of the students felt their non-verbal communication was on point, yet only 38% of employers felt the same.[16] Whether in a job interview or in everyday conversation, there are several non-verbal blunders to avoid:

- Failure to maintain eye contact

[16] Career Center, University of Georgia. www.uga.edu

- Lack of smile
- Bad posture
- Too many hand gestures
- Weak handshake
- Playing with hair
- Fidgeting too much

Professionalism includes learning to say a lot by saying little, and body language can speak loudly without saying a single word.

Representing Jesus

Oh, how great the temptation to just "Be ME!" Countless choices are available for anyone looking for a job or field of study, and some employers are okay with a free spirit who rebels against conforming to a set of rule-like expectations of appearance or behavior. Answering a call to ministry is not one of those fields. Campus ministers are working for an audience of One. Scripture gives a reminder to the person unwilling to grow in professionalism in ministry: *"In those days Israel had no king; everyone did as they saw fit"* comes right from the book of Judges – in two different places. God doesn't demand perfection, but He does ask for excellence in what we say and do. 2 Corinthians 5:20 says *"We are therefore Christ's ambassadors, as though God were making His appeal through us…"* Professionalism is being the best one can be while representing Jesus on the mission field of the college campus.

Cindy Swinney, (B.S.E. University of Nebraska; M.S.E. Doane College) has served on the volunteer staff of Crossroads International since its inception in 2010. Her 30+ years of executive roles in the corporate world give her a unique perspective into ministry. She enjoys building relationships with international students, coordinating events and retreats hosted for area church and campus ministers, and being a cheerleader for international student outreach across the US. Cindy founded a speaking and teaching ministry, New Creations Ministry, in 1994 to encourage and challenge women in their spiritual walk with Christ. Lincoln, Nebraska is home to Cindy and her critters, Ace and Bella.

Chapter 5

NETIQUETTE

Professionalism in Media, Technology and Cyberspace

By Cindy Swinney

It's a made-up word but packed with importance in the life of any professional. Campus ministers face a bigger challenge in this area than those in any other field at the time this book is written. Why? Men and women in campus ministry, especially those coming right out of college, are surrounded by technology. The most obvious is the cell phone, followed by iPads, laptops, tablets, MP3 players, X-Boxes, Fitbits, iWatches… and the list goes on and on. Toss into the mix all of the means of social media interwoven into these gadgets like Facebook, Twitter, Instagram, YouTube, Vimeo, Flickr, Linked In, and blogs galore. Suddenly the mixture has the capability of becoming toxic to personal relationships and professionalism. The campus minister is not only engulfed in technology, but nearly everyone with whom he communicates has the same "stuff."

In striving towards professionalism, how does one navigate through the maze of gadgets to have real communication with real people? How does one fight the pull of the keypad and instead embrace looking up and around at human faces and emotions?

The example to follow is Jesus. Would He have sent a text message to Nicodemus that night to share the words of John 3:16? Would He have snapped a quick picture of Mary as she lay in the dirt helpless at His feet surrounded by men with stones? Would Jesus have captured a quirky video of the money changers at the temple and posted with His comments about His disgust and anger?

While technology can be a useful tool in campus ministry, it can never replace personal contact. Attitude, behavior, and communication are equally important components of professionalism when using technology as they are in day-to-day, face-to-face interactions with others.

Cell Phone Communication

No one denies that a cell phone is a necessary tool for a campus minister. There is a point, however, when this amazing piece of technology becomes a hindrance to ministry work. When phone conversations and text messages become the primary means of communicating, relationships suffer and professionalism is out the window. In her article for Relevant Magazine, Kristin Tennant writes about the social graces missing when constantly on a cell phone.

While technology can be a useful tool in campus ministry, it can never replace personal contact

"I was out for dinner with a friend when I noticed a couple at the next table—she was holding her phone and rapidly firing off a text or a tweet, while her date dutifully chewed away at his burger. 'How rude,' I thought, 'to be typing a conversation with someone who isn't there when you're sitting across from someone you could have a real conversation with.'"

Tennant found herself immediately wanting to jump on a soapbox and preach about the evils of cell phone technology. She is not alone in observing how *"our addictions to technology, social media and instant gratification are slowly eating away at the most important 'real' relationships in our lives."*[17]

This applies only to other people, right? When you feel the buzz in *your* back pocket, that's different. But it isn't different, because there's always some explanation or excuse when it comes to cell phone use. Tennant says, *"Today's college students, as the first generation of adults who grew up with cell phones, are in a unique position to help shape how we can make the most of technology without sacrificing our face-to-face connections."*

An Applebee's commercial a few years ago hit the nail on the head. It began with a young man, alone on a park bench staring at his cell phone and smiling as he scrolled through his texts and reading Facebook posts. The scene then flashed to a booth, of course at Applebee's, with a group of lively young people laughing with music going in the background and hot wings in their hands. "Now THESE are friends!" was their message.

Cell phone calls and texting will never replace the need for face-to-face conversations

Cell phone calls and texting will never replace the need for face to face conversations. Since phones are necessary, though, it is important to practice good manners when using them.

In her presentation "Professionalism in the 21st Century," Anna Post addressed the concern about inappropriate cell phone usage. When asked *"do you encounter people using their cell phone rudely on a*

[17] Tennant, Kristin. "5 Rules for Tech-iquette." Relevant Magazine. October 26, 2012. (Retrieved from http://www.relevantmagazine.com/life/5-rules-tech-iquette#gVA1ClPw3bTlWK3T.99/)

frequent/occasional basis?" a staggering 89% responded, YES.[17]

Some cell phone etiquette rules people till break may include:

1. Talking too loudly. Enough said.
2. Holding inappropriate conversations in public. Keep personal conversations personal. Offer to call the person back, step outside, or find a quiet place to openly and unabashedly describe that new foot fungus.

The world won't stop spinning if you're unavailable by phone for two hours.

3. Rudely interrupting conversations. It's very frustrating to stand around waiting while your friend, date, or family member gets into a phone conversation on your time.
4. Checking your phone at the movies. Turn off the phone and have a little consideration for the people around you. The world won't stop spinning if you're unavailable for two hours.
5. Loud and annoying ringtones. Few see these sounds as clever or funny or musically savvy, and it only makes the cell phone holder look ridiculous.
6. Disturbing live performances. Nothing makes blood boil more than having art ruined by a ringing cell phone. Concerts, plays, and yes, church services can be ruined for those who set aside time and want to relax and focus on what is happening. And – are you sitting down? – this includes whipping out a phone at intermission to check messages. Enjoy the company of those who are there in person.
7. Location, Location, Location. There are countless locations where "taking the call" is inappropriate and extremely annoying to those around you. Libraries, fast food

restaurant lines, business meetings, or even standing in line somewhere are not places to share your life and problems.[18]

"Rude cell phone use has reached an epidemic," said Jodie Vesey, an etiquette consultant in an article for Relevant Magazine. She offers a summarized set of "Golden Rules" for cell phone users.

- The 10-Foot Rule. If you're using your phone in public, always talk at least 10 feet away from anyone. When you're stepping away from someone you're with to take a call, make sure you're not intruding on anyone else's space.
- Ringers off whenever possible. Phones come with vibrate and silent settings for a reason. "Your phone should never be heard ringing during a class, meeting, job interview, or during a meal," Vesey stated. When your ringer is on, maintain a quiet ring tone and don't use a popular radio hit—not everyone will appreciate a Justin Timberlake remix.
- Avoid multitasking while on your cell phone. The worst perpetrators of this are those who insist on using their phones in the bathroom. No conversation needs to be conducted in there.
- Turn It Off. Contrary to popular belief, just because you have a cell phone doesn't mean you need to be available 24/7. "Take a break from the epidemic once in a while," Vesey said. It's OK to turn off your phone. Say it out loud. "It is OK to turn off my phone." The world won't end if you can't be reached for a few hours, and your voicemail will always pick up any missed calls.[19]

---

[18] BSPCN. "Top 10 Cell Phone Etiquette Rules People Still Break," http://www.bspcn.com/2008/08/14/top-10-cell-phone-etiquette-rules-people-still-break/ (accessed July 2016)

[19] Relevant. "Golden Rules for Cell Phone Users," Relevant Magazine, June 2, 2004 (retrieved from

Bottom line? Treat your cell phone as one of your ministry tools, not as an appendage to your body. People trump technology every time.

Communicating Via Text Messaging

Hand in hand with wise cell phone usage comes the importance of texting manners. Teens love to text, exchanging an average of 167 messages per day according to a 2012 survey.[20] While being renowned for that frequency, those in the 18-24 age range are also avid texters, sending around 1,630 texts per month.

In college, studies show the norm is spending 2-3 hours daily texting friends, and another couple hours on Facebook, surfing, or on Twitter.[21] While this behavior is more and more acceptable on campus, a minister is expected to choose more personal methods when communicating with others. A Bible college student studying to become a campus minister might enjoy sending and receiving rapid-fire text messages as a favorite pastime, but once on the job, it is time to exhibit adult behavior. There are a few hard and fast rules for texting to remember:

1. **Texting while driving**. According to a Harvard University study, cell phones cause over 200 deaths and half a

---

http://www.relevantmagazine.com/culture/tech/features/1921-golden-rules-for-cell-phone-users)

[20] Experian Marketing Services' Simmons Connect. (Retrieved from http://trends.e-strategyblog.com/wp-content/uploads/2013/03/Experian-Text-Message-Activity-by-Age-Mar2013.png)

[21] Watters, Audrey. "College Students Admit to "Shocking" Text Messaging Habits in Class." *Readwrite*, December 2, 2010. (Retrieved from http://readwrite.com/2010/12/02/college_students_admit_to_shocking_text_messaging/)

million injuries each year.[22] Laws are in place to make sure people aren't texting while driving, yet many still do. Don't!

2. **Texting while talking.** It is unbelievably rude when someone appears to be listening yet is texting someone else.

3. **Texting small talk.** Resist the urge to fill time by texting "What's up!" or "How r u?" It is annoying enough in person, and twice that via text messaging.

Chad Ragsdale writes that technology today promises to slow down, simplify, and organize lives, but it has actually made people dizzy and sick from overstimulation. The technology that promises to connect people to the world and to each other can just as easily cut off those things. Rather than fully experiencing life in the real world, men and women are choosing an artificial, virtual world. They are choosing alienation.

Might there be a seed of idolatry in these gadgets?

Can cell phones and computers encourage human flourishing and ultimately glorify God? Or might there be a seed of idolatry in these gadgets?[23] Technology combined with common sense and a focus on kingdom work can be a great tool for ministry. If there is a hint of addiction to technology, ministry work will suffer dramatically and striving for excellence will become fruitless drudgery. A minister must test himself regularly by turning off the cell

[22] Auto Safety News and Expert Insight. "Texting while Driving now Leading Cause of US Teen Death." July 10, 2013. Retrieved from http://safety.trw.com/texting-while-driving-now-leading-cause-of-us-teen-deaths/0710/.

[23] Ragsdale, Chad. "My Theology and my View of Technology." Christian Standard magazine. February 13, 2016. Retrieved from http://christianstandard.com/2016/02/my-theology-and-my-view-of-technology/.

phone for a few hours at a time and putting it out of sight in a desk drawer or pocket. For some, anxiety sets in very quickly which can be an indicator that addiction and even idolatry have set in.

This is such a problem in today's culture that there is a name proposed to define this new form of anxiety disorder. Nomophobia is the intense and irrational fear of being out of mobile phone contact. This term coined in 2010 is an abbreviation for "no-mobile-phone phobia." Consider these statistics from a UK survey:

- 53% of mobile phone users in Britain tend to be anxious when they lose their mobile phone, run out of battery or credit, or have no network coverage.
- Stress levels induced by the average case of nomophobia are on-par with wedding day jitters and trips to the dentist.[24]

A Google search for "how do I break my addiction to my cell phone?" will produce lots of good ideas of how to refocus on people and disconnect from too many hours of screen time.

Social Media

"He totally sub-tweeted my Tweet on Twitter. How passive-aggressive is that? I'm definitely going to block him and change my relationship status just to make him jealous." After overhearing this in a coffee shop, Debra Fileta wrote, *"I realized that a majority of the keywords used to describe this dramatic interaction are words that didn't exist in regular*

[24] Elmore, Tim. "Nomophobia: A Rising Trend in Students," Psychology Today, September 18, 2014. (Retrieved from https://www.psychologytoday.com/blog/artificial-maturity/201409/nomophobia-rising-trend-in-students)

conversation 10 years ago. If I could have somehow recorded this conversation and played it to myself back in 2003, I would have had no idea what in the world it all meant."[25]

At every turn in every day, a social media footprint is leaving a mark. Reuniting with an old high school buddy on Facebook can be fun. Gathering support and even fundraising for a worthwhile cause can be honorable via Go Fund Me. And why not do as a couple from Turkey who decided to exchange their wedding vows on Twitter so all their friends and family could "be there?" Yes, social media has a great impact on our relationships. That is good news! And now for the bad news: social media has a great impact on our relationships.

More and more, people try to replicate real life connections through all kinds of social media. Despite best efforts, nothing replaces a warm embrace, a quick smile, or eye contact that talks without speaking. What better example than Jesus? He touched lepers, looked into the eyes of sinners, and embraced His friends. Ministers, church leaders, and all believers should strive to follow His example while engaging in the world around them.

Another danger of social media is the temptation to engage in self-centered behaviors previously associated with only junior high teen types. Included in the list of new words added to Webster's Dictionary in 2012-2015 are selfie, photobomb, catfish, emoji, and tweet. What I look like. Where I want to

We begin to lose our desire to look out, to ask questions and to put the other person first

[25] Fileta, Debra K. "New Rules for New Media: Loving one Another in the Internet Age." Relevant Magazine, July 11, 2013. (http://www.relevantmagazine.com/life/new-rules-new-media#bG1TvuViMWOlRd5O.99)

be seen. What I want to be like. What I am feeling. What I think about everything. I, I, I, I, and I. Social media offers a stage to put each person in the spotlight at the click of a key, encouraging users to share every move, thought, and feeling.

In Relevant Magazine, Fileta puts it well: *"We enter into a state of self-absorption in which we are more interested in proclaiming to the world who we are and what we are doing rather than taking the time to get to know and engage the world around us. So used to promoting ourselves, we forget to edify, encourage and focus on others. So used to looking inward, we begin to lose our desire to look out, to ask questions and to put the other person first."*

Philippians 2 challenges us to live a life that says "no" to vanity and conceit and, instead, to humbly consider others as more important than ourselves. Jesus, who was by far the best example of relational etiquette, lived a life that put others first. I wonder how His example might affect the way we do social media?"[26]

For the selfie-enthusiast, give those 1,278 close friends a break. Few really care when they read posts like "just set a new personal best for my 10K time #feelinggood" or "rise and grind … 5:30 am, time to hit the gym #disciplined" along with selfies in front of a mirror. Check out personal Facebook photo albums to see if there is an inordinate number of selfies, and do a gut check. Then press the little reverse view arrow on the iPhone to find cool things in the big wide world out there to celebrate …. and that don't

[26] Fileta, Debra K. "New Rules for New Media: Loving one Another in the Internet Age." Relevant Magazine, July 11, 2013. (http://www.relevantmagazine.com/life/new-rules-new-media#bG1TvuViMWOlRd5O.99)

include a selfie face.[27]

Facebook, Instagram, Twitter, Pinterest and a slew of other sites have brought us together, yet simultaneously pushed us further apart. Living in a rule-free zone where no one is required to take personal responsibility for what is said or posted can be tempting and dangerous. Each person is left to determine on their own where the boundaries lie for the appropriate use of social media. For a campus minister, it is even more important because of the example being set for those who are looking for guidance.

Cara Joyner penned an article "Five Questions to Ask Before Posting to Social Media" for Relevant Magazine. Her list in summary is:

1. **Am I seeking approval?** We learn behavior through reinforcement. When I seek validation through something I post and that little red flag starts popping up to notify me of each person giving me attention, it's an addictive reward. If you need to hear praise to find happiness, consider healthier ways to address this issue.
2. **Am I boasting?** Proverbs 16:18 reminds us *"Pride goes before destruction, a haughty spirit before a fall."* There's sharing excitement and then there's bragging. Examine your motivations and walk away before using social media as the adult version of show-and-tell.
3. **Am I discontent?** Are you looking for something "better"? If so, walk away. Others' lives will begin to look brighter than yours and breed bitterness and ungratefulness.

---

[27] Carey, Jesse. "Tweet This, Not That," (Relevant Magazine, July/August 2013. Retrieved from http://www.relevantmagazine.com/life/tweet-not#QHvjLdHG7YReLRJk.99)

4. **Is this a moment to protect?** Not every great moment needs to be shared. In fact, some of the best times are most enjoyed privately. If we suspend the present in an attempt to capture its beauty in 140 characters or less, we sacrifice our experience of the moment itself.
5. **Is it kind?** Our culture tells us it's our right to comment on everything, regardless of whether it was addressed to us and without consideration for how it might affect others. We have been given covered space from which to throw grenades, without requiring us to take responsibility for the weight of our words. Jesus said the world would recognize us by our love. What messages are we sending?[28]

Pause before posting. Take a minute to bring discernment, love and wisdom to each picture and word shared on social media. The result will be worth the wait.

Using Facebook for a campus ministry is a great way to reach current students, high schoolers exploring what is available when they hit campus, and alumni who want to keep in touch. The key to using Facebook is to remember when NOT to use Facebook. Discernment is needed on how best to use Facebook to reach students and some others, but it cannot be the only means of communication for the ministry. How easy it is to have the mindset "EVERYONE is on Facebook!" Not everyone is on Facebook, and many middle-aged and older supporters still see it as a less-than-professional, highly impersonal, and lazy way to communicate important ministry updates.

---

[28] Joyner, Cara. "5 Questions to Ask before Posting to Social Media." Relevant Magazine, January 14, 2014. Retrieved from http://www.relevantmagazine.com/culture/tech/5-questions-ask-posting-social-media#7ucquPQFdtvDr0eR.99

Individuals and churches exploring ways to learn about a campus ministry or to offer financial support, prayer support, or encouragement to a campus ministry staff will likely start with a website search. Keep the ministry website updated with plenty of news and contact information, and use Facebook for day to day activities with students. Each means of social media can be a tremendous ministry tool if used appropriately.

Long before social media, Lillian Eichler Watson, a well-known writer with many years of experience in helping people help themselves, said in 1902 what still rings true today:

"Don't reserve your best behavior for special occasions. You can't have two sets of manners, two social codes – one for those you admire and want to impress, another for those whom you consider unimportant. You must be the same to all people."

Email and Netiquette

The days of handwritten letters are gone, replaced by emails speeding throughout cyberspace and creating a need for discussion on email etiquette. Though email has nearly been replaced by text messaging on the college campus, this method of communication is still the primary channel when professionally dealing with many non-students.

An email address is similar to a personal phone number. Giving someone an email address is letting them know that it is okay to communicate in this way. When someone leaves a voicemail, there is an expectation that the call will be returned promptly, and it is the same with an email. It is considered a common courtesy and professional conduct to respond to messages within 24 hours. It is fine to respond, "I am at a retreat/conference/meeting right now so no time .... I'll get back to you Monday morning." Even if it is necessary to say something like this, it is a response so the person knows he is not being ignored. Despite common practices on a college campus to live and die through text messaging, not responding to an email or voicemail in the real world is downright rude and blatantly unprofessional.

A few guidelines for properly handling emails are:

- Check email at least once a day so they don't become numerous and overwhelming. If there are too many, use a filter and delete them just as easily as getting rid of unknown callers on the phone.
- Tempted to get rid of email altogether? No law says the email is required of anyone, but choosing to go down the no-email path shouts, "Leave me alone!" In ministry or any professional setting, that is not the message to send. An alternative is to be honest with people about a preferred communication style. Give an email address if asked, but add "I find it much easier and quicker to respond to texts, so would you mind reaching me that way?" Remember, not everyone has a smartphone yet.
- Don't use LOL or casual word choices when writing professional emails. Sarah delos Santos says in her article Say This, Not That, "many young professionals struggle with differentiating casual and professional language. Even when there doesn't seem to be a large difference between the definition of two words, make smart word choices. What sounds better — "You're wrong" or "That's incorrect"? By tightening up your professional communication skills, you can

sound more mature and give yourself a boost in the adult world."[29]

- The subject line of an email is the first impression for the recipient, says Anna Post. She adds a reminder of email practices to avoid: EMAILS WRITTEN IN ALL CAPS (it can be interpreted as shouting), tx msg spk, and emoticons.[30]
- It is best when sending email to a large list or a list of people who have no relationship with one another to use "bcc" rather than having the addresses visible to all who are getting the email.
- Remember that no email is private. Any email can be forwarded. And forwarded. And forwarded.

Business Letters

Yes, there is still a need for a campus minister to write an actual letter on a piece of paper, purchase a postage stamp, lick the envelope and put into the mailbox. As long as people continue to live past 30-40 years old, the tradition with which they were raised includes writing actual letters.

Unless you are falsely confident that 20 and 30 somethings will donate money in amounts sufficient to support a healthy ministry, business letters are the primary source of communication for ministry fundraising. Any campus minister who believes that a quick Facebook post asking for donations will result in a check in the mail will

[29] Delos Santos, Sarah. "Say This, Not That: Professional Communication for Smart Girls." *Spire & Co.*, November 17, 2014. (Retrieved from http://smartgirlsgroup.com/spirit/empowerment/2014/11/say-this-not-that-professional-communication-for-smart-girls/)

[30] Post, Anna, "Professionalism in the 21st Century," Online video clip. http://www.bing.com/videos/search?q=anna+post+professionalism+in+the+21st+century&view=detail&mid=D27EC968064F74F3D038D27EC968064F74F3D038&FORM=VIRE (accessed July 2016

soon be looking for a part-time job to subsidize his ministry income. Regular direct mailings with a professional business letter, a one-page newsletter or ministry update with a few pictures, and a return envelope are the gold standard. Writing skills are as important here as when writing a sermon or teaching message.

"To Whom It May Concern" vs "Dear Mr/Ms" used to be acceptable in a business letter, but with nearly anyone's contact information available at a quick click on the computer, take time to research the name of the person to whom the letter is being sent. If still not certain, consider using "Hello" for a less pretentious greeting line.

- **Accuracy matters**. In the ABC's of Professionalism, Cross says it is reasonable to expect some stylistic differences when comparing a traditional letter with an email, but grammar and spelling are not matters of style. The quality of one's writing is a direct reflection on his professional image. Most of all, don't rely on computer technology to fix mistakes like to, two, and too. The days of having a secretary to whom proofreading and typing were delegated are long gone. Many young people are woefully unprepared to write in a professional manner. Find a capable partner who can proofread and critique important communication like fundraising letters, newsletters, and even thank you letters sent to donors. Accuracy matters![31]
- **Plagiarism is always wrong.** Replicating things found on the Internet is so easy that the temptation to steal can be overwhelming. Plagiarism has always been wrong and digital technology does not change that moral principle. A

[31] Cross, Clancy. "Your Netiquette is Showing." *Series: The ABC's of Professionalism,* November 18, 2008. (Retrieved from https://clancycross.com/2008/11/18/netiquette/)

professional respects the intellectual property of another and acts accordingly.[32]

- **Sign your name** so others can read it. Some people think to scrawl a scribbly line with a few bumps is an acceptable signature. An unreadable signature may be fine on a check written on a bank, but take care to sign your name neatly on every business, thank you, or fundraising letter. Sloppiness on an important letter may give the recipient an impression that there is sloppiness in the ministry work as well.

The Internet

Those who invented the Internet hit a gold mine! Did they ever imagine this creation as the ultimate tool for expressing opinions, researching almost anything, conducting business, and providing a relaxing pastime for billions of people? With all the good things come the temptations to one's character when exposed to the sleazy dark side of the Internet. Caution and self-control are always required when online. For the purposes of this chapter, the focus is on how the internet could and should be used properly for those in ministry. "Netiquette" is a term to describe the acceptable behavior on the Internet, and there are standards for manners and professionalism.

There is considerable chaos on the internet

Clancy Cross' article "Your Netiquette is Showing" offers some principles to follow anytime anyone is online:

- Netiquette is for everyone. Network etiquette, like professionalism, does not come equipped with an on/off switch. When people strive toward professionalism, their

[32] Ibid.

actions (including online behavior) must always be consistent with their principles. As a professional, people will be watching you and following your lead. You have the power to influence the culture of the Internet with each email you send, each website you visit, and each blog comment you post.

Honor God with every touch on the cell phone and every click of the keyboard

- Practice the Golden Rule. Behavior in the virtual world should reflect the same common courtesies a professional uses in real life. Specifically, this means to be polite, truthful, kind, even-tempered, thoughtful, accurate and forgiving. Not much else needs to be said.[33]

There is considerable chaos on the Internet. Professionals need to step up and be part of the solution.

A campus ministry that hosts a website should keep it current. If no one is committed to regular updates (once a month or more often), don't have a website. The same manners apply to ministry blogs and Facebook pages. If they are online, they must be current or be gone. An outdated website or FB page can give the appearance that the campus minister ultimately responsible for what is says is lazy or doesn't care. The reality is most campus ministers are spread so thin there is no time for website maintenance. Delegate, delegate, delegate. Find a student who is studying communication or technology and hand off this task. In any

[33] Cross, Clancy. "Your Netiquette is Showing." *Series: The ABC's of Professionalism,* November 18, 2008. (Retrieved from http://clancycross.com/favorites/abcsofprofessionalism/)

event, don't just ignore a webpage that boasts pictures of a retreat from 2010 and nothing more current.

All forms of communication done professionally should reflect the excellence to which each believer is called. Honor God with every touch on the cell phone and every click of the keyboard. Choose excellence.

Living a Life with Excellence

Describing professionalism through discussion on attitude, behavior and communication is but one way to get a grasp of the concept and how it looks in campus ministry. Professionalism is choosing to live a life of excellence remembering that every campus minister, every church leader, and every believer works to please an audience of One. Colossians 3:23 is more than just a reminder; the verse serves as a light for a campus minister's path each day. *"Whatever you do, work heartily, as for the Lord and not for men."*

Cindy Swinney, (B.S.E. University of Nebraska; M.S.E. Doane College) has served on the volunteer staff of Crossroads International since its inception in 2010. She enjoys building relationships with international students, coordinating events and retreats hosted for area church and campus ministers, and being a cheerleader for international student outreach across the US. Cindy founded a speaking and teaching ministry, New Creations Ministry, in 1994 to encourage and challenge women in their spiritual walk with Christ. Lincoln, Nebraska is home to Cindy and her critters, Ace and Bella.

Chapter 6

MY LETTER TO ME

By Greg Swinney

Dear Greg,

So, you said *"Yes"* to Jerry and Clark and Gerald and Ed and LaVern and the rest of the board of that small campus ministry at the State College in Nebraska. They call it "The Lighthouse." The name is as much a hope as it is a location. What an exciting start to a new adventure. I guess I don't need to introduce myself, you know me…because I'm you! I'm writing to you from the future to give you a glimpse of what you are in for. I know you are scared and excited all at the same time right now. You've even heard a few in your family say, *"You're going to do what?"* You might feel like it's a shaky way to begin but don't be afraid. The road twists and turns along the way but the scenery will be amazing.

The Lighthouse Board of Directors - 1988

I'll be honest with you from the start. You have no idea what you are doing. Where to start, who to talk to, how to grow a small or large group; all these things are swirling around in your head. I want to encourage you as you begin – think more about who you need to become rather than what you ought to do.

I know that office you are moving into is tiny (I saw it all those years ago). When you are reading a book you almost have to go out into the hallway to turn the page! In that little space, you will dream big dreams and become a vision-caster. You will stare out the cloudy glass of that drafty window on the west side of the room and develop a philosophy of why you are on campus and then think of ways to persuasively communicate that vision to students, supporting churches and everyone you meet. Challenges will turn into opportunities as you sit in that rickety office chair. It's in that room you will offer pre-marital counseling to dozens of young couples and some of them will become vibrant church leaders and even foreign missionaries. In that modest space, you will help that frat guy get his life on track, and talk on the phone with a concerned parent worrying about their young college student. You will work on lesson plans and discipleship ideas in that small workplace and begin to believe in God's amazing capacity to do great things with what feels like very little.

Fruitful ministry will flow from your spiritual disciplines

Greg, the people around you trust you. They know that you will be a self-starter in your new role, they are counting on it. You need to convince them that there is no quit in you. You are a part of their ministry family and you are in it for the long haul. Please don't see this as a stepping stone on the way to "a real church." The nature of campus ministry will require that you work long and hard hours without complaining. And, you often need to start with almost nothing.

I know you because I am you… You feel like a racehorse at the starting gate and you can't wait to run full speed ahead. Let me share with you some words that haven't been written yet but you will read them in about 20 years from now and they will shape you. *"Ruthlessly eliminate hurry from your life."* (Dallas Willard). Spend these early days devoting yourself to prayer and being sensitive to the leading of the Holy Spirit. Fruitful ministry will flow from your spiritual disciplines. Consistently use a Bible reading plan. Keep a journal. Have an ongoing prayer list. Remember the convicting words of Jesus, *"apart from me you can do nothing at all."* (John 15:4, JBP)

You are going to find a couple of things to be very difficult. Saying "Hello" and saying "Goodbye." Greeting new students every year and going through the "where are you from? and "what's your major" will make you feel like a broken record (I think you understand that term, but don't worry vinyl albums will be returning in about 30 years). It's tough to meet new people. But it's even harder when you have been a part of a student's life for four or more years and walked them through broken relationships, financial failure, difficult college classes, memorizing the Scripture together, maybe performing their wedding and then smiling for a picture with them at their graduation and ….saying "Goodbye." That's tough.

Right now, you feel like a lone ranger. It's just you. No multiple staff are in offices down the hall. No list of volunteers sits on that desk that you just bought at that garage sale last week. You are alone. But as you grow into your role, Greg, you will learn how to help people to buy in and feel responsible for the growth and fruitfulness of the campus ministry. There will be an amazing night in just a few years when a student named Kyle will say, let's start a new outreach on campus, and a guy named Rob say, I think we can take

Mexico Mission Trip Team - 1993

several van loads of students on a spring break mission trip and I'm going to work to see that happen." There will be dozens and dozens of others who will move from saying "I go to CSF" to saying "This is my ministry." Discover new ways to help them own it.

I want to urge you, Greg, commit yourself to be an equipper. Train them to minister. That means spending more time training them to teach a lesson than teaching the lesson on your own. Match their gifts with ministry needs and opportunities. Sandy, is a journalism major so train her to do a ministry newsletter. Spend time with her because before long she will want to do her own university-wide newsletter and her dream is to share her faith with everyone, yeah, I mean everyone, on the campus. And she'll do it through that eight-page newspaper. Involve the music majors in leading worship, even if you want to do it yourself. Inspire them through books, experiences, and encouragement. When Carlos comes to meet with you, train him to preach. Then, when you start doing outreach trips to the prison, he can preach the message in Spanish to the Hispanic prison population. Be ready to stand back in amazement when inmates start coming forward following Carlos' invitation to follow Jesus. Yeah, I know he is from Bogota, Colombia, but on the drive home he will tell you these words, "I thought I came to the USA to learn English, but God had bigger plans for my life, He brought me here to preach the Gospel."

Carlos Varela Preaching his first sermon

Set them free. Unleash them to serve. So many area churches need the vibrant enthusiasm of a college kid who believes that God is able to do anything. Youth group leaders, worship leaders, preaching in area churches, summer camp youth workers. Oh yeah, and take that girl named Diane to church camp with you. She will bring her roommate, Pam. When spiritual discussions begin to naturally happen, resist the temptation to step in and interrupt Diane. I know you think that things are being left out or other things must be said. Trust the work of the Holy Spirit. Diane will

God had bigger plans for my life.

help baptize Pam by the end of the week and you will marvel at how God uses ordinary people in such extraordinary ways.

Greg, can I talk to you a minute about sharing your faith with college kids? I know you have taken lots of Bible college courses on evangelism and apologetics. Your Master's degree in New Testament studies gives you confidence that you can answer the difficult questions. There's just one problem. They aren't asking those old questions anymore. Students on campus don't care about a lot of the things you have been trained to discuss. It's always changing. As you walk with them on campus and play racquetball with them in the Health and Sports Center, you'll begin to get to know them on a personal level and break down the barriers that have been built up around their heart. Talk with them on a heart-to-heart level. Your rehearsed responses to their hurts won't register. Walk with them, cry with them, pray with them, and help them see what God wants them to become. Just have them to your house for supper. That speaks to their heart more than you can imagine.

Laurie Sue

I know you've only been married for a few years. But your lovely wife, Laurie, is your biggest fan. She believes in you and is with you 100% and that makes all the difference in the world. She is learning her new role just as you are learning yours. She will be a discipler of women, a Bible study leader, a cook, a hostess, and an inspirational speaker. Thank her and honor her over and over again.

There will be times in the coming years that you want to quit. The Lord will use her wisdom and gentle words to realign your thinking and point you in the right direction. And there will be times her words of truth will come sharply when she says, "Quit feeling sorry for yourself and get to work, try something new!" In about 30 years, some of her most profound words will come and you need to listen to them. When you say, 'I think I need to quit…" she will say, "I think you need to pray." It will change everything. Always let her know that she is on the top of the priority list and don't be cheap when it comes to flowers, ok?

90% of your ministry is about relationships.

Speaking of relationships, I should remind you that 90% of your ministry is about relationships. You need to respond to the needs and concerns of people with grace and sensitivity. When that student calls in the wee hours of the night and is heartsick over a broken relationship or failed exam, you need to show how much you care. Resist the urge to say, "Well, you should have studied more," or "there are more fish in the sea." Sit with them, listen to them, ask lots of questions. There is going to be a young guy named Sam who will drop by to see you when you are swamped with stuff to do. Stop everything and just sit with him. He is about to tell you that his parents just divorced and the first person he has come to see after leaving the courthouse is you. Walk with him. Put your arm around him and listen to his fears and brokenness with your heart. Those other things that seem so important at the time can wait. Sam will need you. Be there.

In a few years, there will be a new invention. They will call it a Personal Computer. I imagine you will want to scrimp and save to buy one of these. It will make your work much more efficient and convenient. That old Underwood™ typewriter, you know the one with the letter e all filled in? Well, it is going to become an antique. You'll get something else called a cellular telephone in a few years. Both of those inventions will change everything about the way you work and live. Just don't let them change who you are. Avoid substituting virtual relationships with real ones. It's hard for me to describe this to my 28-year-old self, but just do your best to let technology be a tool to use, not a god to worship.

Greg, I know you want to see this group grow and flourish. You will feel discouraged at times. There will be many Bible study gatherings that you stress about all the people who aren't there. They had a night class, they bailed to play on their intramural team, there was a special event on campus, someone invited them out for appetizers at Applebees® (um, that place is not around yet, but it will be), and on and on. Sometimes they just don't show. But those who *are* there need you. Listen to the gentle whisper of the Spirit when you hear Him say, "be faithful with a few and I'll send you more." Numerical growth will happen naturally in the context of spiritual and relational growth. Remember those verses you read that said, "and the Lord added to their number…." That happened naturally in the book of Acts after they met the needs of those around them. It will happen with you, too.

Technology is a wonderful tool to use but a terrible god to worship.

Now when you least expect it, the surprise will happen. It might be in a letter or a phone call, but it will happen. There will be an invitation to leave campus ministry and help lead a church or teach at a Christian university. What an honor! But please, please, remember your calling. For years you have said, the university is the place that shapes the future, the culture, and the world. Remember those words you have preached from dozens of pulpits. I know, the salary will be better, the responsibilities will be less, and the prestige will seem appealing. Just, um….remember your calling.

So you are worried about raising money, huh? Yeah, yeah, I know Jim, the treasurer of the campus ministry, told you the funds in the account will only last two months. You think that a fundraiser hat you are forced to wear just doesn't fit. Why not instead become a friend-raiser? Invite people to a vision, a mission. There are tons of gimmicks out there. Just remember once you start down that track, it's really tough to turn the train around and go another direction. Listen close to your friend, Ed, when he says, "instead of auctioning off a Nebraska Cornhusker football for thousands of dollars, why don't we ask God and His people to join in meeting the needs of the growing ministry?" You are going to be awestruck when that phone call comes with a gift of far above ten thousand dollars, and you didn't ask for it or send out a single letter. It shows the all-surpassing power is from God and not from you.

Reshape your thinking to see fundraising as a ministry and not a burden. You know when you give to a church or ministry what happens in your heart and life? Blessings abound. Invite others to be blessed by being a blessing. Listen to me now. I'm writing from your distant future….you will never miss a meal and your kids will not go hungry. Trust Jehovah Jireh, the Provider.

One day you are going to get a letter. There will be no return address on it. No signature. You will have no idea who sent it or where it came from. Inside will be a crumpled up one-dollar bill. The letter inside will have these words scribbled in shaky handwriting, "It's all I have and I'm sending it to the campus ministry." After you wipe away a few tears, frame the letter and the dollar bill. Hang it in your office and don't ever take it down. Notice it as you walk by it and know that some people are giving all they have so you can do what you do. This is a gift from God.

A one dollar gift – "It's all I have..."

As you meet with other colleagues, you will naturally see how they serve and the programs they are trying. Enjoy that time of friendship but resist the urge to compare yourself with them. You tend to be hard on yourself and sort of see your life and ministry as a blooper reel. Then looking at others you only see their highlight footage. Don't be too hard on yourself. God gifted you and made you to be unique and His instrument. Embrace that and don't try to be something that you are not. Someone told me once that if you lined up all the campus ministers in the world in cars on the interstate highway and let them go; the first thing that would happen is 90% would move over to pass. Competition in athletics and business is great, but in ministry it is devastating. Don't compete with those folks over at BigTime U. Love them as family and do all you can to help them be fruitful.

Your journey begins today. As much as you desire for God to show you what the end of the road looks like, you must walk by faith and know that He will bc faithful throughout the journey and gladly show you the next bend in the road.

The name of this campus ministry will follow you your whole life. The Lighthouse. What a dynamic symbol of campus ministry. One of the seven wonders of the ancient world was the Pharos Lighthouse in Alexandria, Egypt. George Bernard Shaw said, "*I can think of no other edifice constructed by man as altruistic as a lighthouse. They were built only to serve.*" Jesus used this imagery of light to describe our role in his Kingdom. We are the light of the world. Reflecting His Light to show the way safely home. Even in the darkest moments, a Light offers hope and shows the Way. When storms rage and the winds blow, the Light pierces the darkness and points to a calm harbor. Founded on the rock-hard ground, the Light invites the weary traveler to a solid place to stand.

Greg, let your light shine……

Send out Your light and Your truth, they shall lead me;
They shall bring me to Your holy hill
And to Your dwelling places.
– Psalm 43:3 [NASB]

Greg Swinney serves as the ministry facilitator for Crossroads International student Ministries. For nearly 40 years, he has served in campus ministry in one role or another. He has taught on over 60 university campuses. Greg and his wife, Laurie, have two grown children, Beth and Nathan, a lot of international students who call them their "American Mom and Dad."

The Lighthouse just three blocks from my home

Chapter 7

LARGE GROUP TEACHING

By Roger Songer

"Why does the fool pay the sage a fee, if he has no mind to learn?" Prov. 17:16

"I am a campus minister."

"A what?"

"A campus minister."

"Sooo... what's that?"

This one, brief conversation represents hundreds I have experienced just like it. Oddly enough, in nearly every one of these dialogues, if I had introduced myself as the "senior minister of a church," or "a youth minister," or "worship minister," or even a "children's minister," the person on the other side of the conversation would have almost immediately grasped a pretty close approximation of my vocation. Campus ministry, though, proves itself a difficult role to explain—and for good reason. In fact, it is so difficult to describe "campus minister" that even when one campus minister meets another campus minister for the first time, neither one really knows what the other person means by their own terminology. This difficulty in pinning down just what we mean by "campus minister" erupts from the extremely broad spectrum of types of ministry included under that name.

Campus ministries vary greatly in basic structure. This variety includes the following:

- Some campus ministries exist as a "campus church." They provide virtually everything a typical local church offers, with the usual exception of the broad age range within the congregation. However, some of these ministries even have become family churches complete with youth groups and Sunday school programs. Campus ministers who serve here share many similarities with local church ministers with the singular exception of that usually very narrow age range of their congregation.
- Some campus ministries operate as one department within a local church. These church-based campus ministries can provide perhaps the broadest of church experiences with a full range of age groups. Some church-based campus ministries locate most of their activities, services and meetings on the main church's campus. Others meet in university facilities for most of their activities but bring their students to the church's campus for the Sunday worship. Many of these church-based ministries enjoy incredible success. Others find integrating university students into their mainstream church to be quite a challenge. One megachurch in Northcentral Illinois just recently turned over their entire college-age ministry to the local campus ministry which they financially support. This church's college ministry had at one time been immensely successful. But over time, the church found it increasingly difficult to juggle local church ministry with something as specialized as campus ministry. As a broad generalization, campus ministers who work for a local church happily avoid one of the more onerous tasks most other campus ministers spend much of their grinding on—namely, fund-raising.

- Many campus ministries avoid offering a Sunday Worship, offering only one mid-week large group meeting. They may, however, offer small group Bible studies throughout the week. Sometimes, campus ministers who serve in this role find that outsiders may have a difficult time understanding how they can be "ministers" if they don't have a "church."
- And a few campus ministries offer no large group meeting, preferring to work only in the one-on-one and small group contexts. However, this methodology rarely exists within Restoration Movement campus ministries.

Large Group Meetings: The (Almost) Common Denominator

Regardless of structure, the one common denominator shared by most campus ministries is that they offer at least one large group meeting each week. This large group meeting fulfills several crucial needs in the life of a campus ministry. For example, the large group meeting provides the one time in the week when the majority of students involved in the ministry can meet together for a large community experience. Second, the large group meeting provides a venue for both the dissemination of information about important upcoming events as well as recruitment and sign-ups for those events (e.g., retreats, conferences, service projects, mission trips, community outreach, on-campus evangelistic events, special prayer efforts, etc.).

The large group meeting provides the one time in the week when the majority of students involved in the ministry can meet together for a large community experience.

And third, arguably the most crucial role, the large group meeting provides a venue for practical Bible teaching. For most large group meetings, the Bible study/teaching portion of the large group gathering maintains the position of priority. When one considers the amount of time devoted to this, it becomes obviously the most significant element of the large group meeting.

The Importance of Solid Bible teaching in the Large Group Meeting

Although some may feel campus ministry focuses upon the current experiences that university students face and the relationships, they find themselves in, it is much more. No doubt, the teaching material of many campus ministers focuses upon personal experience and interpersonal relationships of college students. Campus ministry certainly does focus on the "now," because our time with the students involved in our ministries is brief. On average, campus ministers have about 2 ½ years of contact with a university student.[34] We must work diligently and intentionally to reach, teach, and train those who invest their time and energies in our ministries.

[34] People standing outside of campus ministry looking in usually (fallaciously) assume that since it takes four years to achieve a college degree, we therefore have four years to work with our students. But the actual average of time we have to influence any student's life tends to be attenuated. Why? Because many get involved with us late in their academic careers; others transfer into our universities as sophomores and juniors; and still others leave the university early. And then one must take into account what I call "free-lance involvement." That is, students who float between various campus ministries and either never settle down in only one or "church hop" from one ministry to another throughout their academic careers.

Also, relationships are the building blocks that make up the foundation of life. We find meaning and understanding in those relationships. As a result, we develop small groups for discipleship, community and growth. But the large group meeting plays a very prominent role in our overall approach to ministering to university students.

The Heart of the Matter

A campus ministry—to be healthy—must find its core, its focus, its foundation and its vision and passion in God's Word. As ministries in the tradition of the Restoration Movement,[35] we understand the real truth and power in the simple slogan, "No book but the Bible, no creed but Christ."[36]

The value of serious Bible study in the large group teaching context has been validated to me repeatedly through numerous stories shared by alumni of our ministry. I have often asked our alumni, "What impacted you the most while you were involved with Christian Campus House at Eastern Illinois University?" By far, the most common answer I receive is, "The Wednesday night Bible Study." Many of our alumni from decades ago have held on to the notes and handouts from those Bible studies, and they still use those materials in their own study as well as in discipling others, teaching Sunday School classes, and leading small group

[35] The Restoration Movement (if you are not familiar with the term) refers to a very large loose-knit fellowship of non-denominational churches and individual Christians. From its inception in the 19th Century, it was a unity movement—holding fast to God's Word as the only rule for faith and practice. If you would like to learn more, I suggest you read Unity in Truth: An Interpretive History of the Restoration Movement, by James B. North. Standard Publishing, Cincinnati, OH. 1994.

[36] Although the gist of this slogan forms a part of the Restoration Movement ideological approach to the Christian life, you will rarely hear it spoken in the form of that classic quotation.

Bible studies in their current home church. I know that our ministry does not stand alone in the pivotal role the large group Bible teaching has played in the lives of our alumni. In querying alumni from other campus ministries across the nation, I have listened to many very similar stories.

Without a doubt, a thriving campus ministry must offer a curriculum that can acquaint each student with at least Bible College-level academics. Time with our students is too brief to include a full theological education. But, the time we do have must be used effectively to train young minds in the content of Scripture. This curriculum includes more than offering mild devotional material or "warmed-over" Sunday School lessons. It must include training them how to study the Word on their own (inductively)[37] as well as guiding them toward the ability to make appropriate application of the Word to their own personal lives.

Obstacles and Frustrations in Large Group Teaching

Nothing that has value lacks cost. This is certainly true of Bible teaching—particularly when it takes place in more of a lecture format. Don't be surprised if the energetic

---

[37] The Inductive Bible Study method involves three steps or categories: Observation ("What does it say?), Interpretation ("What does it mean?"), and Application (How do I apply it to my life?). By far, the bulk of the time spent in Inductive Bible Study should focus on the observation phase. Only by investing adequate time in observation does the earnest student of Scripture avoid the leap from reading the text to asking the question, "What does this mean to me?" In my experience, even the brightest and best of university students find themselves to be dismally inept at genuinely observing what the text actually says. All too often, even as they read the text, they are leaping to meaning and application before they actually have grasped what the author is saying. I recommend that the following time be dedicated to each phase in the inductive Bible study method: Observation = 90%; Interpretation = 5%; Application = 5%. A tremendous little tool for developing excellent observation habits is The Joy of Discovery in Bible Study by Oletta Wald (Augsburg Publishing House, 1975).

and curious minds of university students "push back" on serious Bible teaching. Students may grumble, *"I sit in class all day and listen to teachers lecture. When I come to our large group meeting with campus ministry friends, I don't want just another lecture. I want something fun!"*

From my perspective, if disciples of Jesus take that master/disciple relationship seriously, they should welcome the opportunity to learn—even if that opportunity involves a *"lecture."*[38] So, if your primary teaching method involves a lecture format, and you hear the critical tones emanating from your students about the woes of a lecture format, what do you do?

Research suggests that the millennial generation has neither the heart nor the patience to endure the lecture format. Nor do most of them possess the attention span to remain focused, engaged, and alert for much more than 15-30 minutes.[39] Yet, the millennial generation does not own exclusive rights to short attention spans. Television, the internet, video games, texts, and social media like Twitter and Facebook, have impacted the attention spans of every generation extant in our culture. And I do not see this pandemic of decreased attention spans soon making a reversal.

---

[38] We have to find a way to encourage intentional learning as a discipline. Not to seem "snarky," but Jesus is known for His "Sermon on the Mount"—a monologue, not His "Small Group Discussion on the Mount." Small groups have their place in campus ministry. But so do more intense teaching times in the large group.

[39] The observation of this attenuated attention span constituted a common thread of comment among the 15 campus ministers I surveyed as background research for this chapter.

A Changing Generation

About seven years ago our staff and student leaders met for our annual weekend spring leadership retreat. In our debrief time, the student leaders offered critiques on every facet of our ministry for the current year. When it came time to critique the large group teaching, 75% of our student leaders felt that our teaching time was too long. Oddly enough, the other 25% pretty loudly dissented, insisting that we needed to maintain our current 40-45 (sometimes longer) minute study time. To that majority who were clamoring for a more brief teaching time, I asked this question: *"What is it you would most want from our large group teaching time?"* One of our brightest, most promising female leaders said, *"Lecturing doesn't cut it for me. It doesn't fit my 'learning style.' Instead, I need about ten minutes of teaching. And then I need some good stories. I really need the teacher to tell me how to apply the teaching, and then, I need something 'kinesthetic.'"* Many of our student leaders nodded in agreement.

Although people certainly differ in learning styles, I must confess—the idea that university students would feel the need for a "kinesthetic" (body movement) component in a serious Bible study took me by complete surprise! I thought, *"What is this? Nursery school? Aren't you all supposed to be maturing adults, seriously pursuing an academic degree at a reputable university? Do you really have to be led in some sort of physical activity to drive home the point of a Biblical teaching?"*

Our ministry staff discussed this evaluation of our large group teaching for months. We wrangled over it. I personally agonized over it. But, there was no avoiding reality. We realized that we were ministering to a very different generation of students. Tim Elmore has aptly written about this age group in his must-read book Generation i-Y.[40] Our staff embarked on a pilgrimage to discover new ways of reaching students through the large group teaching. We continue to find new wineskins that more aptly carry the wine of the gospel to this generation.

The Problem of Biblical Literacy

One of the real issues we face in campus ministry is, "How do we navigate through waters of shortened attention spans towards a destination leading to Biblical literacy? Anecdotally, and analytically, an all too real case can be made for the dismal state of Biblical literacy among those who claim to be Christians.[41]

Mike Luzadder, campus minister at East Tennessee State University stated the problem accurately and bluntly: *"We [American Christians] are still largely Biblically illiterate—too much fluff in youth group, methinks. I do believe that those students coming from Christian Churches are better prepared than others (Church of Christ students are usually exceptional; mainline churches border on the ridiculous), but they are all still largely unchallenged."*

Some ministries have moved to multiple mini-series in teaching

[40] Generation i-Y: Our Last Chance to Save Their Future (Poet Gardener Publishing, 2010). If you have not read this book, please order it now! Elmore will open your eyes to the "why?" behind a whole host of issues you may be facing with current college students, recent alumni (and high school students).

[41] The Barna Group has produced reams of statistical material assessing the current state of "the Church."

Negotiating the Obstacles on the Path to Biblical Literacy

In preparing to write this chapter, I surveyed fifteen of my peers who serve in campus ministries across the country. One of the questions in my survey asked about the length (in minutes) of their large group meeting, and how much of that meeting time was dedicated to the actual teaching time. The total time carved out for the large group meeting ranged from fifty minutes to 1 ½ hours. The time dedicated to the actual teaching ranged from the shortest (fifteen minutes followed by 15-20 minutes of small group discussions) to the longest at 45-55 minutes (presumably a lecture format). All fifteen responses to my survey pretty much agreed that any teaching lasting beyond 20-30 minutes begins to radically impact current students' maximum attention spans.

Another question for my peers focused on what these veteran campus ministers had found to work best in their environment concerning length of series (e.g., year-long?, semester-long?, multiple mini-series?, or no series at all?). Some of the fifteen who responded regularly plan a large group teaching curriculum in semester-long series. None of them teach year-long series. Most of the fifteen responders indicated that they had moved to multiple mini-series teachings in order to capture and maintain their students' interest and involvement.

Inviting to Something More

When our ministry staff began strategizing how we could best reach this generation through our large group teaching time, we had to ask and answer— "Who decides the curriculum?" "Who formulates the methodologies for teaching God's Word?" If the prevailing attitude of students asks for fun, for brevity, and for mostly discussion-based studies, do we capitulate to their felt needs—their *wants*? And if we do, how do we use the large group teaching to challenge them to rise above a culture that lends itself to ignorance, immaturity and shallowness? How do we invite them to ascend to 1) deep understanding, 2) a pattern of spiritual growth, and 3) greater depth in a foundational understanding of Biblical truth?

Paul's warning to Timothy may apply to our situation on campus, "*...the time is coming when people will not endure sound teaching, but having itching ears they will accumulate for themselves teachers to suit their own passions... .*"[42] In context, Paul's concern focused primarily on people who turned from the truth of God to myths. However, Paul might also be equally concerned about the current trend in our culture for disciples to turn from solid teaching to fluff.

> *Is my responsibility as a teaching minister to give the people what they want or provide for them what they need?*

Perhaps we must take a different approach even if that approach leaves some students longing for "fluff"—knowing full well that those who want the "fluff" may leave our ministry in search of another ministry that will give them what they want. That was (and still is) our dilemma in campus ministry. At the end of the day, the ultimate question becomes: is my responsibility as a teaching minister to give the people what they want or provide for them what they need?

If you serve in vocational ministry and your giftedness is in teaching, you have an obligation to prepare your life and message at a level that, when you teach, you are calling God's people to a deeper walk with Him as well as to a higher, more

[42] 2 Timothy 4:3 (ESV)

developed standard of processing the truth of Scripture. The writer of Hebrews admonishes the readers to move from milk to meat. This is our Biblical mandate; this is our hope.

I would caution you, if you take too harsh a stand you run the risk of insulting and alienating genuine disciples of Jesus. A gentle compromise of these two methods is where our staff decided to hang their hat. We teach in shorter series, and we restrict our total meeting time to one hour. This includes announcements and a time of some inspirational worship.

When we want to teach a series that must last an entire semester, we do not necessarily label it with a theme. For the most part, the students come, listen, and absorb, unaware that we are in a series that will last the entire semester. This gentle compromise helps us meet our teaching objectives, while at the same time, remaining sensitive to students' needs.

Key Elements of the Large Group Teaching

Here are some of the most important elements that must become a part of the large group teaching—and especially must be grasped by the one *doing* the teaching.

Foundation

It should go without saying, but what you teach needs to be the Word of God. Assume students are hungry and seeking. Feed them real food, not junk. Avoid this temptation: "I have a really good idea of what I would like to teach. I know my topic, now I will go to the Bible and look for some good sounding verses that will drive home my point." Instead, begin with the Word, and let your message flow out of the fruit of your study of that passage.

James warned, *"Not many of you should become teachers, my brothers, for you know that we who teach will be judged with greater strictness."*[43] Anyone who assumes the role of teaching God's Word needs to wrap his or her brain around this very real warning. God views your teaching as a serious undertaking with a serious purpose and with serious implications. You should, too. So, when you teach, teach the Word.

Vision

Clarity. Purpose. Results. Life-change. When the large group teacher possesses vision, these become the focus of what gets taught. Visionary teaching presents Biblical truth with great clarity—not confusion. Visionary teaching knows its purpose, which is not entertainment nor merely the dissemination of raw information. Our students do not need more information. They can get more information than they can ever digest just by searching the internet on any given theological topic. What they desperately need is someone who can teach them what to do with the information they gather—to focus on the purpose of knowing the Word.

What do I want them to do, think or change?

When you teach, do you constantly have in your mind the purpose you want to accomplish? Hand in glove, purpose and results fit together. If you know your purpose, then you should have a clear idea of the concrete results you want your teaching to produce. And as you cast that vision, you will know that what you want your teaching to accomplish is life-

[43] James 3:1 (ESV)

change. Sin, laziness, lethargy, apathy, and ignorance[44] run rampant in the lives of university students. Visionary teaching calls the hearer to accountability and repentance. Continually ask yourself, "what do I want them to do, think, or change, as a result of this message from the Scripture?"

Preparation

Anything worth doing is worth doing well. When you teach in the large group setting, the moment is too valuable—the time too precious—to cheat your listeners by offering them anything other than your very best. And lack of preparation dooms your teaching to be less-than-your-best. Here are some guidelines for preparation:

First, time knows no substitute and tolerates no rival. To be adequately prepared to teach in the large group setting you must spend sufficient time in preparation. A good rule of thumb is that you should spend at least 30 minutes in preparation for every minute you spend speaking. So, a thirty minute teaching deserves about fifteen hours of preparation. Can you get by with less prep time? Probably. Will you be giving your teaching your very best? Only you can answer that one.

Second, methodology does matter. The way you prepare will directly influence—even drive—the way you teach. If you prepare by searching the internet for a pre-packaged lesson you can copy, or adapt and then teach, you are not prepared. You are cutting corners and may even be guilty of downright, blatant plagiarizing.

The methodology needed to teach most effectively involves total personal immersion in the passage which forms

[44] Ignorance is not a synonym for "stupid," nor is it an insult on one's intelligence (IQ). Ignorance is the lack (or rejection) of knowledge and understanding of important truths.

the basis of the lesson. You must spend enough time in your passage that when you do teach, you are not presenting what you were barely able to scrape together from the bottom of your intellectual barrel. Instead, you will teach from the overflow of your preparation—the cream that rises to the top and spills out over the sides. How do you get to that state of immersion in the Word? Through inductive Bible study.[45]

Simply put, inductive Bible study moves you through three stages: observation, interpretation, and application. Guess which of these stages holds the status of undeniable priority (in terms of the time you spend and the energy you invest)? *Observation*. But what do most Bible studies (large group, small group, or individual) commonly hold up as their ultimate goal? *Application*. The problem is that if you have not spent quality time observing what the text actually *says*, you really have no foundation for talking about how it can be applied. Interpretation and application without the hard work required in observation tend to lead to a misuse or abuse of the Word. If you have not yet learned and become adept at inductive Bible study, let me recommend to you the following short book: The Joy of Discovery in Bible Study, by Oletta Wald; Augsburg Fortress Pub., 1975. Many books have been written on this subject, but this one is brilliantly concise. It also contains a chapter and a chart on observation that are simply outstanding.[46] Once you become adept at genuine observation, you will be stunned by how wide-open God swings the doors of your heart and the windows of your mind to understand His Word in a way you never have before!

---

[45] Much of the content of this section is also mentioned in footnote #5.

[46] Suffice to say, the scope of this chapter does not allow me space to completely unpack the inductive Bible study method. But let me encourage you. If you buy Wald's book and invest your time and energy in learning the method—especially the observation phase—your Bible study (personal and public) will be revolutionized.

Precision

Accuracy counts. The large group teaching requires the teacher to possess a drive for correctness. Words and their original meanings matter. Grammar matters. Syntax matters. Context matters. Many of you reading this chapter might be astounded to know that you have been misusing Scripture by taking verses out of their context. Would you enjoy a couple of test cases? Here are two passages that I find well-meaning Christians chronically misusing because they do not understand the context in which the verse falls:

First, in Matthew 18:20 Jesus says, *"For where two or three are gathered in my name, there am I among them."* Typically, Christians will apply this by claiming, "Where two or three are gathered together, that constitutes a church." Or, they will say, *"If two or three of us pray together, God is with us in a special way—more special than if we prayed alone."* Nope! Wrong! In Matthew 18 Jesus teaches a process for dealing with a brother who has sinned (or sinned against you). In the middle of this process, he instructs them, *"But if they will not listen, take one or two others along, so that 'every matter may be established by the testimony of two or three witnesses.'"*[47] The "two or three" in verse 20 derive their identity and dynamic from the "two or three" in verse 16—the immediate context. What Jesus is teaching is this: In the process of conflict resolution in the body, where sin is involved, two or three people (witnesses) should gather to collect information (testimony) from both the "sinner" and the "corrector." Then these 2-3 "witnesses" are prepared to serve as arbiters in the situation. They will judge (discern) who is telling the truth and who is not concerning the alleged sin. The promise Jesus offers in verse 20, then, is that *"...when two or three (witnesses) gather in "my name,"* I will be with

[47] Matthew 18:16 (NIV)

them to give them the wisdom to discern and arbitrate a solution between the unreconciled brothers." That is the meaning of verse 20. Any other use of the verse violates context… precision denied; error accepted; shame on me.

For the second example, in Philippians 4:13 Paul writes, *"I can do all things through Christ who strengthens me."*[48] Many people simply shorten the quotation simply to "I can do all things through Christ." In my experience, most Christians believe this is some sort of promise from Jesus that anything and everything I *need* to do or *want* to do I *CAN* do, simply because He has promised me success. So, the verse comforts many people who are not good at ______ (fill in the blank) and believe that Jesus will give them success. Conversely, the verse creates a neurotic dissatisfaction in many people because they believe that Christ will enable them to do whatever they set their mind to (e.g., run a 4 minute mile, or lose 50 pounds this year). So, for far too many believers this verse becomes a perfectionist's whipping post to which they tie themselves. Imagine how they feel about themselves and about God when the "promised" success does not come?

Again, the truth is found in the precision of the context, and here it is:

"…I have learned to be content whatever the circumstances. I know what it is to be in need, and I know what it is to have plenty. I have learned the secret of being content in any and every situation, whether well fed or hungry, whether living in plenty or in want. I can do all this through him who gives me strength.[49]

[48] Philippians 4:13 (NKJV)
[49] Philippians 4:11b-13 (NIV)

As you can clearly see from the context, Paul declares that he has learned the *"...secret of being content in any and every situation."* When he continues by proclaiming his ability to *"do all this through him who gives me strength,"* he speaks directly of practicing contentment in his current situation whatever that happens to be—rich or poor, hungry or satiated. Not one word Paul writes here encourages his readers to aspire to achieve the impossible, the improbable or the unlikely. He in no way guarantees that Jesus promises to make you well-fed when you are hungry, rich when you are poor, or a world-class athlete when you are simply not capable of such prowess. In essence, verse 13 means exactly the opposite of its common usage.

Welcome those who check up on your precision. You need to develop a culture in your teaching in which those who learn can go to the Word on their own to determine if what you are teaching is accurate, correct, and faithful to the Word. After all, Paul lovingly lauded the Bereans as being more faithful than the Thessalonians, because they *"...searched the Scriptures daily to see if what Paul said was true."* If Paul loved the Bereans' quest for truth and precision in his teaching, who are we to expect anything else of those whom we teach?

Passion

What your students need to see in your teaching is what burns in your heart. They need to see how Scripture grabs at your heart, molds your mind, refreshes your spirit, directs your will, and shapes and empowers the whole of your personal life and ministry. Be careful though; don't ever confuse a manufactured enthusiasm with genuine passion. Your students can spot a phony, forced enthusiasm—and they will reject both your artificial passion and your message.

Jeremiah, the Weeping Prophet, famously wrote, *"But if I say, 'I will not mention his word or speak anymore in his name,' his word is in my heart like a fire, a fire shut up in my bones. I am weary of holding it in; indeed, I cannot."*[50] When a passage of Scripture captivates your heart and sets it ablaze, let that heat warm the hearts of your students. Your passion will be contagious. The fire in your heart will light a fire in theirs. ON the road to Emmaus the disciples said, *"did not our hearts burn within us while we were with him?"*

They searched the Scriptures daily to see if what Paul said was true

Illustration

Teaching in a large group requires more than merely exegeting the text. Accurately explaining the text only begins the teaching process. If you do not bring meaningful stories or illustrations to bear on the main points of the teaching, your audience will not likely be moved to action nor will they remember what you have taught. I stated earlier that this generation connects with stories as a part of the large group teaching. They are not alone. In fact, everyone needs Biblical truth to be fleshed out through story. Jesus was, and is, admired as the greatest of storytellers. When confronted with hard questions by his adversaries (even questions rooted in Old Testament Scripture), Jesus routinely answered through story or parable. Effective use of pertinent stories and illustrations relevant to your text makes the message come alive. Be on the lookout for stories in the news, online, and from personal experience that can add fresh application to the words you are teaching.

[50] Jeremiah 20:9 (NIV)

Application

An apt teacher practically applies the text by offering examples of how it fits in the lives of those listening. But, on the other hand, those who are taught bear a great deal of the responsibility for listening intently to the teaching, assimilating the information, understanding the challenge, and then responding to the call to action by figuring out *for themselves* how the passage can best be applied in their life circumstance. Providing an exhaustive list of possible applications of any passage of Scripture he or she teaches for every listener is not possible. What the teacher needs to provide is the motivation and the challenge to his or her audience to dig into the passage on their own and make the appropriate application. Suggesting life-changing action is simply where a teacher begins, it ends with the listener. It may be the teacher's goal. It may be the teacher's great hope for the listeners. Ultimately, only God, by His Spirit, can provide the interface between the Word and the human heart and thus produce fruit.

God's Work through Earthen Vessels

Large group teaching forms a powerful, integral, essential dynamic in campus ministry. What God does with your teaching is *His* great work. How we prepare for our teaching role is *ours*. Knowing that the fruit that our teaching produces depends on both *His* operation and *our* cooperation, accept the challenge and the comfort found in Paul's powerfully encouraging words . . .

"Now to him who is able to do immeasurably more than all we ask or imagine, according to his power that is at work within us to him be glory in the church and in Christ Jesus throughout all generations, for ever and ever! Amen."(Ephesians 3:20-21).

Roger Songer, (Rose Hulman Institute of Technology, 1971-72; B.S., Lincoln Christian University, 1976; M.A. in New Testament, Trinity Evangelical Divinity School, 1979) began campus ministry in 1973. For 38 years Roger served as campus minister (Oklahoma State University, 1979-1984; Eastern Illinois University 1984-2016-retired). Roger and his wife, Sue, live in Charleston, IL, and have three grown daughters and six grandchildren.

Chapter 8

uWORSHIP

By Matt Stafford

When we speak of worship today most likely we immediately think of music. While music is certainly a fundamental aspect of Christian worship, worship is much bigger than music alone. Scripture offers the best guidance when it comes to a foundational understanding of the nature of genuine worship.

You won't find Jesus' primary teaching on worship in one of his sermons or in one of his conversations with his disciples. Surprisingly, Jesus uttered his most profound words about worship to an outsider, a foreigner, a woman, a social outcast who misunderstood worship but was willing to learn (John 4).

About mid-day, Jesus' disciples had gone into the town of Sychar to get some lunch. Meanwhile, Jesus stayed outside the village and sat down by the town's well. As a woman approached the well to draw water, Jesus surprised her by asking for a drink. His request violated several social taboos and generated great curiosity in the mind of the woman. After a brief exchange about water in which Jesus suggested that he could offer water that's better than the water of the well, Jesus created some discomfort by bringing up the woman's past. She admitted to having no husband, but Jesus went on to reveal, she had been divorced five times and was now living with a man. We don't know the circumstances of those broken relationships, but we can assume she lived each day with wounds on her heart. Jesus didn't condemn her or focus on her past. Instead, he affirmed her honesty even as she had been trying to hide the truth. Realizing that Jesus is a prophet, that is one who listens to God and speaks truth, she decided to ask him to settle a burning theological question related to worship.

For centuries, her people, the Samaritans, had worshiped God as Moses had commanded, on Mt. Gerizim. The Samaritans were devoted to the law of Moses which said nothing about worshiping in Jerusalem. They stuck to the teaching of the first five books of the Old Testament, the Law of Moses. The Jewish people, on the other hand, had additional scriptures and a history of temple-based worship in Jerusalem since the time of David and Solomon. She wanted to know Jesus' opinion on "the right way." Listen to his answer:

Genuine worship can take place anytime and anywhere

Jesus said to her, *"Woman, believe me, the hour is coming when neither on this mountain nor in Jerusalem will you worship the Father. You worship what you do not know; we worship what we know, for salvation is from the Jews. But the hour is coming and is now here when the true worshipers will worship the Father in spirit and truth, for the Father is seeking such people to worship him. God is spirit, and those who worship him must worship in spirit and truth."* (John 4:21-24, ESV)

In his kind response, Jesus couldn't be clearer. The Jews were right and the Samaritans were wrong, but the good news was that it really didn't matter anymore. Three key principles about worship emerge from this text.

Worship is not about Geography

Genuine worship can take place anywhere and anytime. The temple and religious festivals were soon going to be a thing of the past, and Jesus was about to usher in an entirely new kind of worship. His people would no longer need to go to a temple on a holy day to offer sacrifices and pray, for his people would become the temple itself. Paul makes this clear in his letter to the church at Corinth writing, "*Do you not know that **you are God's temple** and that God's Spirit dwells in you? If anyone destroys God's temple, God will destroy him. For God's temple is holy, and **you are that temple***" (I Corinthians 3:16-17, ESV). Lost in translation is the fact that the "you" in this text is plural. Paul makes it clear that the church is the temple. The community of believers is now the place where God meets with his people. Thus, one of the roles of a worship leader is to help the worshiping community understand and experience the presence of God wherever they might be. Worship doesn't require a building and it doesn't require the latest high-tech audio and video gear that we assume are essentials for modern worship. In fact, those tools, as powerful and helpful as they are, can often get in the way of authentic worship. In our pursuit of the ultimate musical worship experience, we've got to be careful not to leave the presence of God out of it. Don't miss opportunities to lead your students in worship outside of the typical campus setting. Go outdoors, set up on the campus quad, grab a guitar and gather around a campfire or worship on a porch. Think outside the building. God doesn't live in temples built by men (Acts 17:24). He lives in the hearts of His people, the church.

What is true on the corporate level is true on the personal level as well. In the same letter, Paul later writes, *"or do you not know that **your body is a temple of the Holy Spirit***

***within you**, whom you have from God? You are not your own, for you were bought with a price. So glorify God in your body"* (I Corinthians 6:19-20, ESV). The backstory of Paul's instruction here is that individuals in the church were following the cultural norms and engaging in sexual immorality. Such behavior is incompatible with the new life in Christ. The call of this text is to personal holiness. If your body is a temple of the Holy Spirit, then it needs to be a holy place, set-apart and unpolluted from the world.

> *What you do on stage is almost as important as what you do offstage*

Those who assume the role of worship leader in a campus community must embody this reality and strive to live a life of utmost purity. Anyone who is on stage is seen by others as a leader, and that means (like it or not) they are held to a higher standard. College students are quick to spot hypocrisy in others, and a lifestyle off stage that doesn't match the words spoken on stage will quickly undermine leadership. Remember, what you do on stage is almost as important as what you do off stage.

God is Seeking Worshippers

Secondly, Jesus went out of his way to speak to the Samaritan woman. His mission statement was, *"to seek and to save the lost"* (Luke 19:10). In his parable of the prodigal son Jesus portrays God as a father who is longing for the return of his son, running to him with open arms when he finally comes home. Jesus said, *"No one can come to me unless the Father who sent me draws him"* (John 6:44). There's no question that God is actively seeking worshipers. The last thirty years have seen an emphasis placed on seeker-driven and seeker-sensitive worship, designing our worship gatherings to be attractive to those outside the faith. I think this has generally been a positive movement to engage our culture as it is, rather than ask culture to bend to conform to our traditions. However, it's critical to remember that God is seeking people to worship him. We cannot make people worship. Too often we think that if we get the environment just right, select the perfect songs, and arrange them in dynamic and creative ways, then we can create transformative worship experiences for the community. While those things are important, they do not make people worship. This removes a tremendous burden from worship leaders who feel that they have to get everything just right for worship to happen. God has always been calling people to Himself. The role of a worship leader then is simply to partner with Him in issuing the call.

Worship Him in Spirit and Truth

God is spirit, that is, He exists and operates beyond the physical realm. Theologians call this "beyond-ness" of God "transcendence." I remember Don DeWelt saying, "the prayer closet is where the world that we live in meets the world that we believe in." Worship takes place in the space where those worlds come together – the physical and the spiritual. To worship in spirit is to acknowledge the reality of a spiritual realm that is beyond sensing and then to align our lives with that reality. To worship in truth is to affirm what we know to be true about God from reason and revelation. In a post-modern world where truth is considered relative to one's experience and perspective, we must resist the urge to fit into our culture and instead shape our worship around the revealed truth of God. There is a truism that tells us that we become like that which we worship. If we worship material things, we become like them – hollow, empty, lifeless. If we worship ourselves, we become more selfish, arrogant, and lonely. In speaking of idol worship, the psalmist wrote, *"Those who make them become like them; so do all who trust in them."* (Psalm 115:8, ESV)

Because worship transforms us, the object of our worship is critically important. Worship without the spirit is dead orthodoxy. Worship without truth is sappy sentimentality.

Romans 12:1-2

A second foundational text about worship is Romans 12:1,2. The theme of the book of Romans may be summarized in this phrase from its first chapter: *"the gospel is the power of God for the salvation of everyone who believes: first for the Jew, then for the Gentile*" (1:16) Paul then expounds upon that statement until the end of chapter eleven where he is so overwhelmed with the glory and beauty of what God has done that he pauses to worship. Worship begins with his doxology in 11:33-36, *"Oh, the depth of the riches of the wisdom and knowledge of God!"*, and it continues into chapter 12 where he writes, *"I appeal to you therefore, brothers, by the mercies of God, to present your bodies as a living sacrifice, holy and acceptable to God, which is your spiritual worship. Do not be conformed to this world, but be transformed by the renewal of your mind, that by testing you may discern what is the will of God, what is good and acceptable and perfect"* (Romans 12:1-2, ESV).

Worship is Rooted in the Gospel

Worship is motivated by the *mercies of God*. It is a reasonable response to the gospel, and thus the content of worship must be centered in the gospel. The story of Jesus and the acts of God in history and in our story are the bedrock of worship. Our preaching, our singing, and all other acts of worship must be infused with the gospel message. The gospel is the power of God and it is the fuel for worship.

Worship is Sacrifice

Paul uses the language of sacrifice as this was readily understood in both the Jewish and Gentile world. In the ancient world, worship always involved sacrifice, in the same way, today most assume that worship must naturally involve music. When a citizen of the ancient world heard the word "worship," they probably didn't think about music. They thought about sacrifice. When they went to the temple, it wasn't to sing or be sung to. They came with an offering. Paul is expanding the concept of sacrifice by calling worshipers to bring not a material offering, but rather, their very lives. So not only is the believer a temple where God dwells, but the Christian is also the sacrifice offering in that temple. The act of living a life surrendered to God is an act of worship. When the community gathers to worship, the call is not just to sing, but to sacrifice.

When the community gathers to worship, the call is not just to sing, but to sacrifice

Paul says that this presenting of our bodies as a living sacrifice is our *spiritual worship*, or more literally translated, our *reasonable service*. In other words, it is the rational response to the sacrifice of the body of Christ for us. It is a logical exchange. In the worship assembly, we are confronted with the reality of God's sacrifice for us, and the most appropriate response on our part is to sacrifice ourselves for

Him. Do our worship services compel us to this kind of devotion? They should.

Worship Results in Transformation

Genuine worship is a shaping experience of non-conformity to the spirit of this age. The gods of our culture exert tremendous molding pressure upon us. The values of western culture – individualism, unlimited sexual freedom, and materialistic excess – seem so natural and normal that we forget that they are antithetical to the gospel. If worship is spiritual transformation, what are our worship services transforming us to become? Are they renewing our minds, molding us into a new community that shares a radically different set of values? Or does the pattern of this world shape our worship? These are the questions that worship leaders should be asking.

Having laid a foundation of governing principles regarding biblical worship, let us now turn to consider the corporate worship service itself. The New Testament gives us a window into the worship practices of the nascent church, practices that have endured to the present. These include preaching (2 Timothy 4:1), the public reading of scripture (1 Timothy 4:13), prayer (Acts 2:42; 4:24; 12:12; 1 Timothy 2:1-8), giving (1 Corinthians 16:2), the celebration of the Eucharist (1 Corinthians 10: 14-17; 11:17-34), and singing (Matthew 26:30; Acts 16:25; I Corinthians 14:15; Ephesians 5:19; Colossians 3:16; James 5:13; Revelation 14:2-3). Worship leaders would do well to think deeply about all of these worship practices, rather than merely focusing on the musical aspects of worship. If we don't, we may find ourselves placing the accent in the wrong place, and offering a skewed worship experience to our students.

Historically speaking, church practice has distilled the worship service itself down into two primary elements: word and table. The "word" is that portion of the worship gathering where the congregation listens to the Word of God. This takes place in the form of preaching, the reading of Scripture, and the singing of biblical truth. God speaks to us through His word and we speak back to Him and one another in our singing.

The "table" portion of the worship gathering is variously called the Eucharist, the Lord's Supper, and communion. It is the remembering of the body and blood of Jesus in the act of eating bread and drinking wine together. Whether one takes a sacramental or a symbolic only view of communion, the fact remains the New Testament has more to say about this act of worship than any other. The table serves to bind us together as a believing community (1 Corinthians 10:14-17; 11:17-22); it continues a practice that Jesus Himself commanded us to observe (1 Corinthians 11:23-25), and it is a non-verbal proclamation of the gospel (1 Corinthians 11:26). Participating in this aspect of worship in an unworthy manner invites the judgment of God (1 Corinthians 11:27-34). Collegiate worship leaders will encounter a variety of views regarding the Lord's Supper, so it is important to be both sensitive and instructive. Referring frequently to the texts above in a worship gathering reminds us of the centrality of this meal and the proper ways in which we are to participate in it. Careful explanation of this meal is particularly important for outsiders to whom the practice may seem strange.

Let me write the songs of a nation; I don't care who writes the laws

Although it is only one aspect of worship, the role of music in the corporate worship experience has become preeminent in recent years. Scottish parliamentarian Andrew Fletcher is credited with saying, *"Let me write the songs of a nation, and I don't care who writes its laws."* His statement speaks to the power of music and song to transform cultures. The worship leader wields that kind of power in the writing, selecting, and leading of songs. In the past, Christians would recite their creeds in the worship service. Now we sing them.

Leading corporate worship involves three primary activities: planning, preparation, and implementation.

Planning for Worship

Prayer should always precede planning. It is an acknowledgment of our dependence on God, a means of keeping us humble, and a way to access wisdom from God in leadership. I believe that God will guide the worship leader in planning as an overflow of their own personal worship experiences. It is significant that the book of Psalms, a prayer book that teaches believers how to worship, begins with a call to find wisdom in personal worship. The psalmist writes, *"His delight is in the law of the LORD, and he speaks aloud the word of God day and night. He is like a tree, planted by streams of water, fruitful in season whose leaf does not wither, and whatever he does prospers."* (Psalm 1:2-3, *author's translation*).

Devote significant times in the worship service to the reading of Scripture

The Scriptures

The Bible should form the backbone of the worship service. Sometimes the text or theme of the sermon will direct the selection of songs. In this way the sermon and the singing support one another. Worship leaders may also plan a service around a particular Scripture text, typically one of the psalms, selecting songs whose lyrics coincide with the passage of Scripture. When selecting songs, leaders must examine the lyrics to see that they are biblically accurate and theologically sound. In the service itself, plan to read the Scripture texts aloud, inviting the congregation to join. The Psalms are a great place to begin because they offer a wide variety of liturgical content. They have been the basis for much of the worship of believers for the last 3,000 years, and worship leaders should learn the language of prayer and worship through disciplined reading of these prayers both publically and privately. Devote significant amounts of time in the service to the reading of Scripture. The Word of God is living and active (Hebrews 4:12) and has the power to transform those who listen.

Selecting Songs

Biblically rich, musically accessible, and emotionally powerful songs are the most transformational. Because music is such a powerful tool for memory, it's vitally important that we sing songs that are worthy of remembering. We've all had the experience of wanting to get a song out of our head. Devote a great deal of thought to selecting songs for worship that will linger in our heads and hearts long after the singing is over. Songs should be biblically rich in that they contain a great deal of Scriptural content. I ask my worship leaders to give me chapter and verse for every line that they sing. Songs should paraphrase scripture in memorable ways and state sound theology that is grounded in the Word of God. Because of the power of song to transform, there is no excuse for singing songs that express weak or misleading theology.

Accessibility of Song Selection

Songs should also be **musically accessible**. This may seem obvious, but the beauty of singing together is that everyone is singing *together*. If the song is pitched in a key that it too high for the majority of people to sing, if the arrangement is not easy to follow, if the melody line is covered by aggressive instrumental music or even vocal harmonies, the worshipers will stop singing in frustration. Participation is one of the primary goals of worship leading, and this is an area where musicians need to submit to the congregation they are serving. There are times when it is appropriate for worshipers to be still and let the music and lyric wash over them, but this should be the exception rather than the rule given the abundant commands in the Psalms to "sing to the Lord" (Psalm 95:1).

Plan with a Creative Team

The second word in the Hebrew Bible is *create*. We worship a creative God and we are created in His image. That includes His creativity. Just as God created in community (the trinity), so we also create best in community. Even the most creative person eventually will run out of ideas, and a certain synergy takes place when students creatively plan for worship. Creative planning sessions should welcome any idea, regardless of how impossible it may seem at first. These often spur other ideas and help to get the creative juices flowing. In creative planning, I've found it helpful to move past the obvious. In other words, reject the first idea that comes into your mind, and force yourself to look for others. You may come back to your original idea, but more often than not, you'll come up with something far better. Think about ways to involve the worshipers in the service beyond singing. Consider how to involve all five senses in the worship experience.

Preparation

In most college ministry settings, the large group gathering for worship is led by a team, so musical preparation is required. This means that a band and vocalists, as well as technical personnel, are necessary to create the needed audio and visual environment. Student leaders need to prepare music, develop arrangements, and rehearse the team, all of which require a certain level of musical expertise. Excellent music requires rhythmic tightness, attention to dynamics, and variety in instrumentation. These all require time and practice to develop. As a musician, the goal of practice is to achieve automaticity – the ability to play and sing without thinking about the mechanics of playing and singing. If you are focusing on where your fingers go to make the shape of the chord, or if you are thinking consciously about your breathing while singing, you are not going to be able to focus on the lyric you are singing. Strive to be so well prepared musically that you can fully engage your mind in the content of what you are singing.

Spiritual Preparation

Authentic worship leadership requires spiritual preparation as well. It goes without saying that leaders need to be consistent in practicing the spiritual disciplines of the

Christian life. Richard Foster's, Celebration of Discipline, is a great place to start. Foster describes thirteen classic spiritual disciplines in three categories: the inward disciplines of meditation, prayer, fasting, and study; the outward disciplines of simplicity, solitude, submission, and service; and the corporate disciplines of confession, worship, guidance, and celebration. Regular, balanced practice of these disciplines promotes spiritual growth and serves as a foundation for effective leadership. Sometimes worship leaders will insist that their role is primarily musical, and thus, the spiritual disciplines are not as important as musical excellence. However, the role of a worship leader is primarily that of a teacher, utilizing music and song to teach the truths of scripture essential to the spiritual formation of the community. Music is simply a tool for teaching, and worship leaders need to be growing spiritually before they attempt to lead the spiritual growth of others.

Implementation

As a worship leader, one of the greatest compliments I ever received came from a friend who said, "When you lead worship, you simply disappear." That's not a bad way to describe the role of worship leader on stage. Yes, we must speak and lead, and we must play and sing with skill, but when it's all over, the important thing is that the attention and adoration went to God and not to an individual or the team on the stage. Humility is thus an essential quality of a worship leader.

Leaders need to be growing spiritually

Effective worship leaders are also adept at communicating with the congregation. Carefully constructed comments, clear instructions, and authentic prayers at the right moment can lead a community into a conversation with God. Leadership like this flows out of one's own personal worship and practice of the spiritual disciplines. If you are being spiritually fed every day, you will have something with which to feed others. Speak with a confidence born out of prayer, preparation, and the conviction that you are called to lead in this moment. Rest in the promise that he who called you is faithful (Hebrews 10:23)

Finally, worship leaders need to be pastors at heart. A pastor is a shepherd, and a shepherd knows his flock. When you are leading worship, often your eyes will be lifted up to God, singing to him. Other times your eyes will be closed as you focus your thoughts on God alone. However, you must also set your eyes upon the people before you. You look out and see Kimiko whose parents have disowned her because she has become a Christian. You see Mike and you know he is struggling with a chronic illness. You see Becca in the back lifting her hands to God, remembering that just last week you stood by her at the funeral of a friend who took her own life. You glance at Caleb and think of his struggles with addiction that he's shared with you in counseling sessions. Every face in the room has a story. Knowing those stories and seeing God's faithful hand in each of them broadens your worship of God as well. It is said that when Billy Graham got up to preach, he did so with the realization that there is a broken heart in every pew. The same is true when we lead worship. The better you know your faith community, the better worship leader you will be.

Matt Stafford is the Director of Worship and Creative Arts at Ozark Christian College. In his 35 years of college ministry, he has focused on worship leadership, discipleship and spiritual formation.

He has concentrated his academic study on the Psalms, publishing extensive resources at mattstaffordpsalms.com.

Chapter 9

CAMPUS MINISTRY'S INVOLVEMENT WITH HOUSING STUDENTS

by

Greg Swinney & Dave Embree

> **Rooms for Rent:** Christian Student Fellowship is accepting applications for residents to live in a distinctly Christian setting. Call mornings....

During the 1960s, '70s and '80s, many upstart campus ministries purchased old houses on the edge of the campus in which to hold Bible studies and perhaps have an office or two. Often the houses had spare bedrooms, which were then rented out to students to help cover the cost of the facility and to start building a core of involved students. In recent years, the impulse of new ministries to immediately invest in facilities has not been nearly so strong.

In January 2016, a survey was emailed to over 100 members of the Association of College Ministries to ask about their experiences with housing students. Fifty-four individuals provided feedback among whom 53% of their ministries offered housing for students, ranging from a few who offered living space for one or two all the way up to ministries which house 85-100 students. The majority of ministries offering housing have been doing such for a long time—52% more than 21 years, with another 37% falling into the 6-20 year range. Only 3% of the responding ministries have been offering housing less than 5 years. 90% of those presently offering housing stated that if they were to start their ministry all over, they would provide housing again. But of those responding to the survey who did not presently offer housing, hardly anyone indicated they were at all interested in adding that to their ministries.

What makes housing students worthwhile? According to this survey, the most significant benefit of student housing is the opportunity to develop the authentic Christian community it provides. Other positives include enhanced opportunities for discipleship and accountability. Several ministries cited leadership development as a perk, and others noted that housing created deeper ties between students and their ministries.

Given the challenging spiritual environment on university campuses, one might assume that creating a more wholesome, affirming haven might be a major factor in offering housing, but only a few ministries suggested that reason. On the other hand, several ministries noted that communities of students attract other students, creating central points of outreach. Student housing was called a "ministry hub" by some reporters, who also noted that such facilities provided opportunities for students to offer hospitality to others, host small groups, and hold social events. Engaging residents in ministry was seen to be a major outcome.

The costs of a university education continue to escalate, and providing quality housing to students at reasonable rates was offered as a significant benefit of offering residential facilities. But relating to finances, the additional income that housing can provide for doing campus ministry actually ranked as the second most commonly cited benefit of providing student housing. Indeed, some campus ministries are very significantly funded by their housing units.

So what are the downsides of housing? The time and financial pressures of keeping up and enhancing facilities were ranked as the most noted drawback. But sometimes the roles of "landlord" and "pastor" can be in conflict with one another, and that tension was frequently mentioned. Conflict and tension among housemates and the drama that produces were also commonly cited as troublesome. Other respondents noted that disciplinary issues and disregard for covenants and other commitments were on-going issues.

Their overall assessments in offering housing is that the positives outweigh the negatives

Despite the many ministry benefits noted above, other campus ministers noted that drawing influential leadership people out of university housing often reduced their potential impact on campus. And, though students living in ministry housing tend to draw very close to one another, sometimes it becomes difficult to keep non-residents feeling as much a part of the ministry. Occasionally, bad enough conflicts arise through ministry housing that the result is long-term bitterness towards the ministry.

But, among campus ministries offering housing to students, their overall assessment is that housing students offers positives that far outweigh the negatives.

Campus ministry boards, campus ministers, and supporting congregations have failed to reach a consensus regarding the issue of housing students. The problem is not a new one. As read in the chapter on the history of campus ministry, a trend throughout the 1970s emerged. A regional board would establish a base of operations, but due to the high cost of property adjacent to university campuses, the best that many could manage was to purchase a moderate-sized house (usually a single-family dwelling) and set up shop.

The base of operations allowed for office space, limited meeting space, and a visible point on campus to call home. If indeed this was a single-family house, it came complete with a kitchen, bathroom, and a few bedrooms. Only needing the living room for small group meetings and one or two other rooms for office space, renting rooms to offset ministry expenses often seemed like the thing to do. It just made sense to use the space to its fullest capacity. The majority of Christian Church campus ministries have adopted this method as the norm. But not without problems.

Irresponsible or apathetic residents, tax laws and endless maintenance tasks have the potential to soak up a campus minister's time. These issues, as well as others, have kept the jury in continuous deliberation over the topic of campus ministry's involvement in housing students.

This chapter seeks to provide the reader with information, both pro and con, regarding this issue. The opening section of this chapter discusses the advantages to campus ministries housing students. The second section details the disadvantages. The chapter ends with some practical suggestions.

YES

Offering housing to students desiring a Christian atmosphere really isn't a bad idea. Missionaries working in third world nations sense the needs of the people and move to meet them. They make food available, provide educational services, and strive to meet basic necessities. Campus ministers feeling the pulse of college life realize students have a basic need of finding suitable housing. Why not move to meet this need and offer a distinctly Christian alternative?

I remember when Sally came to visit me. She had been sleeping in her car for the past week. I remember that morning because she looked like I felt--very tired! She described her roommate as a "tramp." Even though Sally continually voiced her displeasure to her roommate, she only got an "if you don't like it, move out" response. Many universities, like ours, require freshmen students to live on campus. Moving out was not an option for Sally, so she slept in her car.

The last straw was when Sally, with her mother, stopped by her room to pick up a few things. They walked in on Sally's roommate in bed with not one but two college boys. That was it. When she came in to see me she literally begged for a place to stay. Raised in a Christian home, she knew if you lived in a cesspool long enough, you'd start to smell that way yourself.

Sally had been sleeping in her car for the past week

One room was available and Sally sacrificed her expensive dorm deposit and moved out before the semester's end. She found fellowship with other Christians and often expressed thanks for "letting her move in." Later, when other students would complain about a leaky sink or a drafty window, Sally always kept gratefully quiet.

1. The most valuable reason to have student housing is to **offer a distinctly Christian environment** for students to call home. We view it as a specialized ministry, a support group, a safety net. Living in a Christian atmosphere for 24

hours a day, seven days a week is not an opportunity many find. Campus ministries without a resident housing ministry can have tremendously successful ministries, but when a situation arises for "intensive care" they come up short.

Over the years I have ministered on our campus in Nebraska, we have caught dozens of students in our safety net of housing. I could fill several pages of this chapter with stories of countless others like Sally. A common situation is a young person leaves home, gets to college, and finds himself in a living situation (in college housing or otherwise) that would be defined as immoral, even degrading. Like the prodigal son, they "come to their senses" and realize they must get out. Seeking godly counsel and the help of other Christians, they turn to ministries that can meet that need of housing. Indeed, not all students seek this option, but many do. Campus ministries which house students can offer that twenty-four-hour-a-day accountability group. Others cannot.

When students from our college transfer to another university, a common question they ask me is, "Do you know of a campus ministry there with a campus house. I want to live with Christians."

We view this housing facet of our work as a specialized ministry. Yes, it's tiresome and, at times, stressful. It's costly and time-consuming. But....it's fruitful.

2. The second advantage to housing students is the **foundation of special friendships**. Of course, people can find friendships without living in a campus house. This is true. Still, students living in this environment become friends quickly and remain friends forever.

I conducted a wedding recently where the bride (one of our campus house students) especially requested the presence of all her "old roomies." Thirty-five attended. I could easily sense the bond they felt with one another was extraordinary. That level of friendship is formed only by living together as they had. In the future when they look up the word "friendship" in the dictionary, these students will see a mental picture of roommates there at the Christian Student Fellowship.

3. A resident housing ministry also offers a **unique effort in evangelism.** The primary purpose of our housing ministry is for "mutual edification and nurturing of Christian brothers and sisters."

However, at certain times, an opportunity to evangelize students avails itself to our housing ministry. Some people express shock and say, "You let non-Christians move into a Christian housing ministry...supported by churches?!?!" Wait a minute. Let me explain.

"I want to live with Christians..."

When a student comes to us and expresses a sincere search for answers in life, we talk with them. They share with us their need for help, direction, and guidance. Our students meet, interview the individual, and discuss the matter. They pray about it, sometimes for several days. If they feel they can be of assistance in leading this individual along his or her spiritual pilgrimage, they invite this student to move in. Sometimes this is on a temporary or "provisional status" basis. This type of effort is completely organized by resident students. It's their call. In this situation, the more mature residents are "extra sensitive" to the needs of this newfound friend. Discussions surrounding ultimate Truth and Christ's commands often go into the "wee hours" of the morning at the campus house. Exposure to these discussions and the caring atmosphere found among the students is life changing.

The successes of such situations are staggering. One student came to a single Bible study, observed the climate of this magnetic fellowship, and confided in me afterwards. "My life is a mess, I can't straighten it out alone, I need help. Can I move in with these other Christians to get my life back on track?" After consulting with the Floor Shepherds (our counterpart to the Resident Assistants of the dormitories), he moved in. Within two months he was baptized into Christ and began making noticeable changes in his everyday lifestyle. I'm certain that the network of Christian friends in this housing arrangement was instrumental in his decision.

An international student came one day, "I want to learn how Christians live. Is room open?" There was and he did. Today, somewhere in Rio de Janeiro, Brazil, there is a Christian businessman managing a clothing store. He saw how Christians lived and wanted it for himself. I still remember the tears in his eyes the day he moved out. "Come visit me in Brazil," he said, "you can live with me."

Of course, there are dangers with efforts of this nature. Desperate and homeless students may make up any story to get a place to stay for a while. However, once again, the 24 hour a day spiritual boot camp they find themselves in either gets through to them or they go awol. We always trust the Lord's Word will never return to Him void, even when we feel we have sometimes failed.

4. **Financial assistance** for ministry expenses is another blessing of housing students. We have housing available for 22 students (eleven male and eleven female). Our rate of occupancy is about 95%. In an average academic year, we have a waiting list of half a dozen students. Some put their name on our list as long as two years in advance. The Lord blessed us with abundant rental income this past year--

$24,000. Interestingly, our annual report showed that after building payments, insurance, utilities, repairs, and miscellaneous property expenses, we had a net gain of only $300. You say, "That's a lot of work and a hefty investment to make three hundred bucks!" Consider renting 10,000 square feet of meeting space within 100 yards of the university. You'll pay $3,000 per month. Don't be too hasty. Any ministry worth doing well involves a lot of work and expense.

We enjoy 3000 square feet of meeting space that is "free" to us. To rent that space near the campus would be at least $1500 to $2000 per month. We would be hard-pressed to raise that kind of money to have meeting space for our exclusive use throughout the week. Since we have it though, we enjoy it. The extra space provided by our housing outreach is used for a Christian library and resource center, a fellowship kitchen used for graduation and wedding receptions, and very comfortable office accommodations.

We work hard to be less and less dependent on this income for programming expenses. Godly board members prayed hard for wisdom to understand the financial aspects and demanding responsibilities accompanying a resident housing ministry. They determined a "break even" point. Currently, we need to house fourteen students to balance the books on the property. Still, our leaders are committed to never compromise our ministry by letting economic crises rule in the decision-making process.

Our board knows the housing is not our source of income, the Lord is. If tomorrow the housing ministry became ineffective, we would reassess, shift gears and try another approach. If necessary, we would sell and trust the Lord to bless our efforts. If ministry on this campus for the past twenty years has taught us anything, it has taught us flexibility and the need to quickly adapt to any given situation.

5. Housing students makes for **good relations with area churches** since they see personal needs being met. Sad to say, some people in some churches are more willing to give to an effort in which they see personal benefit. It's only natural. Families with children approaching college age see the dire need for a wholesome alternative to dormitory living or, worse yet (gasp), fraternity houses. They pray for and contribute to our ministry because they see how we are meeting basic needs their son or daughter may soon have.

Families with children approaching college age see the dire need or a wholesome alternative to dormitory living

As I visit churches, people ask me, "Is the house full?" Their thermometer measuring how hot or cold our ministry is rises and falls based on the number of residents we house. That's discouraging! Even when our campus house enjoys 100% occupancy, I respond to these friends by saying, "Oh, we've got some great students living with us," then lead them on to focus on another aspect of our ministry's fruitfulness by adding, "but let me tell you about something else going on that really excites me...."

6. Housing students **makes parents happy**, I mean really happy. When their son or daughter tells of the atmosphere found at Christian Student Fellowship, most parents breathe a prayer of thanks. Parents know the staggering influence of friends and neighbors, not to mention roommates. One loving dad told me this is the kind of place

for which he had been praying. He had prayed for months his son could find a place to live like this.

Although some parents disagree with our theological stance, they thank God for us because we are one of the few ministries on our campus to meet this need. They believe in us. Last year I was reminded several times how one family felt that we had been an answer to their specific prayers. So, despite doctrinal differences, parents continue to support us financially, seeing our need-meeting mindset.

Further, we have found that if one student from a family lives with us, younger sisters or brothers are often future residents. In four or five different families, younger family members have moved into our campus house because their older brother or sister had such a growing experience here.

Yes indeed, housing students can be a very effective avenue of campus ministry. After discussing the problems and headaches of housing students, our Board of Directors looks to the lives changed and glory the Lord receives because of it and says, "How blessed we are to be able to offer this--it's worth it!"

NO

When both Christian Campus House at SMSU and I were young, we proceeded to do what we knew campus ministries among Christian Churches were "supposed" to do: to provide housing for students. Indeed, before I was hired, the board had purchased a house adjacent to campus in which to house students. However, someone had not done enough research, and the board found that the house was not zoned for housing multiple students, so when I came, my wife and I moved into that house, and soon thereafter the search began anew for a facility to serve as student housing.

Why were we so committed to housing students? Southwest Missouri State University was growing rapidly at the time and was incapable of providing enough housing to meet student demands. Further, students told horror stories of "dorm life" and we thought it would definitely be a legitimate ministry to rescue young people from such an atmosphere. But the most significant reason for me, though I would never have admitted it at the time, was that somehow I felt housing would validate our ministry as "having arrived." The "flagship" campus ministry in our state was at the University of Missouri at Columbia. Housing had been a part of their ministry almost from the very beginning. MU students told wonderful stories about how much living in Christian housing had uplifted their lives, and even with all the student housing available at MU, they always had a waiting list for semesters ahead. If the ministry at SMSU was going to be "big time," we needed housing and the sooner the better.

The plan seemed simple enough. We would purchase a large home near campus, renovate it as needed, and create a Christian community where godly love would ensure harmony and spiritual growth. We studied the real estate ads in the paper and combed the neighborhoods around campus to find just the right place.

Suddenly all the right pieces came together. Within a period of about a year and a half, we found a house that could be remodeled into housing for nine women. A Christian businessman offered to lease us a house in which we could house 12 or more men. Then a local church purchased some land and offered to let us house six or eight students in the home that stood on their new property. We went from housing no students to the capacity of housing around twenty-five. We were a real campus ministry at last!

Though the houses did not "take off" quite as quickly as we had anticipated, we enjoyed some immediate benefits. Our ministry looked much more like the most well-known campus work in our state. Parents began to contact us to find out about our housing. The first students to move into our houses loved the experience of living with other Christians with whom they could have good times. When each week's Bible studies rolled around, we knew that the atmosphere would get exciting when all our house residents showed up. Some residents built deep and close relationships with other residents that endure to this day. I was able to spend good discipling time with the young men in the men's house.

Housing students takes a major commitment of time and money

Housing students takes a major commitment of time and money. Many people contributed both to get our houses operating, but the free labor ran out long before all the necessary remodeling was done. The financial gifts helped make down payments and covered much of the cost of renovations, but the theory was that the houses should pay for themselves operationally. None of these ever did. Consequently, as the campus minister who was responsible for the houses on a day-to-day basis, I spent a great deal of time physically working on the houses, recruiting assistance to maintain the houses, and figuring out how we could make the houses pay for themselves while not charging rents so high that people could live much more inexpensively elsewhere.

We recruited mature Christian students to serve as head residents of each house, who lived there for half price in exchange for dealing with rent, utilities, and such and for serving as peer counselors. The head residents and I found that many financial, personal, and relational situations demanded a great deal of time and effort from all of us. Often our ideals of a harmonious Christian community in each house were undermined by students who were uncommitted to Christ and/or uncooperative with anyone who held ideas about how they should behave. Instead of dealing with issues of assisting one another to mature in Christ and meeting mutual needs, house meetings tended to deal with unpaid phone bills, unwashed dishes, and unmet expectations. I felt less and less like a spiritual mentor and more and more like a referee and landlord. On-campus visiting of students, preparation for teaching, and creative outreaches to other students took a back seat to trying to make the houses work right.

The reader can probably suggest solutions to many of these problems. "You should have been more selective in your interview process." "You expected too much of college students." "You should have recruited more help to take care of the daily operations." All these statements are true. But the lack of finances forced us to, at times, to house people we suspected might be disruptive; we did not expect more than basic Christian responsibility towards one another; and at eleven o'clock at night, it was much easier for me to run over to unclog the toilet than to try to find a board member to do it. We definitely made many mistakes, and it was one of the toughest times of my ministry.

In 1984 we decided the lease arrangement with the men's house was not working out at the same time the owner did. The church which had allowed us to use their house for students decided to turn it into office space. A major developer decided to build a condominium tower on a site partially occupied by our women's house, and, after several city council hearings, was given the right to do so despite our protests. We went from housing for twenty-five to housing for zero more quickly than we had obtained it. Despite the frustrations shared above, our first response was, "What are we going to do? Our housing is gone!" We were not using any of the facilities for meeting or office space; all our programs other than housing moved ahead unhindered. However, we still felt housing was such an integral part of "correct" campus ministry that we immediately began to search for other student housing. We had learned that we wanted to do many things differently, but we began nearly immediately to look for another housing facility.

After two years of examining many properties in the university neighborhood, making offers, and watching houses we had considered being razed for parking lots, we began to think the unthinkable: maybe we could run a campus ministry without housing. Since losing all our housing, our ministry had started to grow numerically. I was finding time for one-on-one discipling, and our corporate stress level plummeted. We felt financially secure enough to hire a female staff member. Our outreach and campus orientation increased significantly. We moved our large group Bible studies to campus. For the first time ever, the number of on-campus students involved with our group surpassed those of off-campus students.

Since losing all our housing, our ministry had started to grow numerically

We ended up buying a new house--for offices and small group meeting space only. The house is open during the day and evenings for students to hang out, study, eat, and sometimes nap. Our students all feel equally that the house is theirs. Our staff offices are also located in the house and can be locked up separately. Lots of our students still live together, rooming together in the resident halls, or renting apartments together off-campus. They enjoy as much community as they want; they pay their own bills; they call their own landlords. We still help people deal with roommate problems regularly, but we don't worry about them walking out of our house leaving us with unpaid bills!

I know this sounds entirely negative regarding housing, and probably somewhat whiny. Sorry. We have considered housing a few times in recent years but never pursued it far. We have decided that if we were to try it again, we would seek apartment-style housing, which would minimize group conflicts and direct cleaning responsibilities. Such a setup would also be more flexible in responding to varying demands for housing. We would also not want to be economic hostages to our housing, needing to keep it full just to keep finances on an even keel. We would also write much tougher contracts than we ever did before.

As for me and my (campus) house, we have decided that we can be a real, legitimate, need meeting, servant training, fellowship enhancing, Bible teaching ministry without it.

Some Recommendations and Suggestions

1. If you go with a housing ministry, think of it as just that -- a ministry. Viewing it as a business will make you begrudge time spent in fixing that broken light fixture or complaining when the stool overflows. See it as a ministry to students.

2. Check your motives. If you pursue a housing ministry to "keep up with the Jones'" campus ministry across campus or across the state at "Bigtime U," you will be miserable. This

effort is a labor of love. Without the motive of love, the labor involved can become overwhelming.

3. If you choose not to go with housing, don't berate or criticize those who do. They work hard. You don't appreciate criticism after hours and hours of hard work on a project; neither do they.

4. When considering a property that may be used for rental usages, remember the three keys to real estate: location, location, location. Property in a high traffic walk-by area is the only place to be. Resist the temptation to buy the cheaper, smaller place down the street. You won't find residents, and if that's one of your intended sources of income, you'll be in trouble. Oh yes, and check the zoning of the area before you buy.

5. If you decide to house students, do it right, "as unto the Lord." Buying cheap and fixing things halfway will not only make it difficult to rent; it will also tarnish the image of your ministry. You'll be seen as the people who don't care, probably because you don't.

If you are currently housing students but feel you are doing it poorly, walk through the house and rooms. If you would be embarrassed to invite one of your favorite relatives to live there for a month, maybe you've got some remodeling to do.

6. Involve students in key house leadership roles. Give them the responsibilities in selecting incoming residents and policing themselves concerning the rules. Require regular house meetings for devotions, interaction, and prayer. These meetings have the potential to become "gripe sessions," so

prompt student leaders to direct the discussions towards positive ends.

7. Make the rental agreement specific and demanding. Resist the temptation to compromise and lower your standard to just “fill up the rooms."

8. If you choose to get out of housing, consider organizing alternatives. Begin a "Roommate Connection" ministry to help match up Christian students. They can live and mature in a nurturing atmosphere, building solid relationships.

The Conclusion of the Matter

To house or not to house? That is the question. Many ministries have found housing to be an integral part of their successful programs. Every campus is different. If it is working in a given place, praise God! If it is ineffective in other places, try something else; don't do housing because it's the thing to do. So the answer to the question of to house or not to house is a definite "Maybe."

Dave Embree began serving as campus minister with Christian Campus House at Southwest Missouri State University in 1978. His undergraduate studies include time spent at Ozark Christian College and Southwest Missouri State University, from which he received a B.A. in Antiquities. He has done graduate work at SMSU and Cincinnati Bible Seminary. Dave also teaches in the Religious Studies Department at SMSU. He and his wife, Joyce, are the happy (most of the time) parents of daughters, Catrina and Christina. Dave enjoys outdoor adventures, discipling students, and writing.

Greg Swinney led the Christian Student Fellowship at the University of Nebraska at Kearney, NE for 26 years. In his years of ministry there, the housing ministry of students grew from four residents in a broken-down house to twenty-two residents comfortably housed in a $500,000 facility. He hates plugged toilets, leaky faucets, and malfunctioning appliances, and would much rather be preaching than plunging. About the housing ministry to students, he says, *"I've never had a headache this big that brings me so much joy."*

Chapter 10

DEVELOPING INTERNSHIPS

By Roger Songer

"...when you're alone, you're in bad company..." (Jean-Paul Sartre)[51]

He began alone. Jesus, that is. Alone. Led into the desert by the Holy Spirit, Jesus faced bitter temptation at Satan's whims in the midst of a grueling 40-day fast. Living alone among wild beasts, He found His only comfort from the angels who ministered to Him.[52] Secluded, assaulted, famished, yet strangely energized, Jesus emerged from this stressful time in the desert, returned to his home territory of Galilee and immediately began his earthly ministry. His message? "Repent, and believe in the Good News!"[53] Jesus began his earthly ministry at the age of 30. And he was alone.[54]

Starting out in campus ministry can create a personal life experience much like that of Jesus. If you begin in campus ministry without multiple staff, you feel alone. Painfully, you will sense Satan's subtle temptations, and your

---

[51] Please note: In using this quotation, I am not hinting that Jesus Himself is in poor company in his "aloneness." The reference is intended to set the tone for what follows as we begin to talk about the value of adding interns in order to share ministry, rather than to work alone.

[52] Mark 1:13

[53] Matthew 1:14-15

[54] "Alone" in the sense of without a human partner in ministry. Of course, His Father and the Holy Spirit were his constant companions. But, he began ministry without an earthly, human helper.

own hungering spirit will ache to be filled in the emptiness of an oppressive "desert." And, although you will not likely live among wild beasts, you certainly will experience real fear erupting from the often hostile culture of the secular university—the very mission field God has called you to reach.

Solitary ministry can drain you. Danger lurks in the aloneness

When I began in campus ministry, loneliness, fear, and spiritual hunger often overwhelmed—even oppressed—me. I felt alone. Speaking to this very dilemma, the author of Ecclesiastes wrote: *Two are better than one, because they have a good return for their labor: If either of them falls down, one can help the other up. But pity anyone who falls and has no one to help them up. Also, if two lie down together, they will keep warm. But how can one keep warm alone? Though one may be overpowered, two can defend themselves. A cord of three strands is not quickly broken.*[55] Applied Wisdom cries out, "Solitary ministry can drain you. Danger lurks in the aloneness. But sharing ministry offers the beneficial power of comradery, mutual comfort, mutual support, a united front in the face of danger, and heightened productivity."

Enter . . . Internships

Because two are better than one, I am a huge fan of internships. Adding interns to ministry staff can enrich your own personal and spiritual life by providing a vehicle to share the load and the loneliness of campus ministry.[56] Interns add amazing value to your organization and provide tremendous

[55] Ecclesiastes 4:9-10, 12 NIV
[56] Cf., Galatians 6:2

opportunities for growth and practical experience for the interns themselves. But what, exactly, is an "intern?" Webster defines intern as "a student or recent graduate who works for a period of time at a job in order to get experience." For the first five years of campus ministry, then at Oklahoma State University, I served alone.[57] We employed no multiple staff and no interns.

Why Interns?

Interns can be found in many walks of life: In state and federal government working for members of congress. In the business world, working for major corporations. Even in show business, working on the crews of popular television programs. You can also find "interns" working alongside journeymen laborers such as electricians, welders, plumbers, and carpenters. Typically, this class of "interns" we call "apprentices." In fact, a great synonym for "intern" is "apprentice." And it is not a coincidence that "apprentice" is also a synonym for "disciple"—Jesus' chosen term for his followers. The word, "disciple," means, literally, "a learner." In an academic setting like campus ministry, we too easily fall prey to an incorrect understanding of what this kind of "learner" must be. We quickly and erroneously often equate discipleship with "scholarship"—learning facts and knowledge—like a college classroom experience. But in Jesus' day, "disciple" did not find its

Our staff had grown into "graduate internships"

[57] Well, not exactly "alone." My wife, Sue, served admirably while also tackling the role of a full-time mom. But I was the only full-time campus minister during my tenure at OSU. Many of us in the earlier years of campus ministry relied heavily on our wives for moral and spiritual support, as well as for help with the detailed work.

definition in a person who learned facts and theories; a disciple learned from the model of his master by doing what his master did.[58] Discipleship was a mentoring experience. Jesus ministered alone only for a very short time before he began to issue the call for men to become his disciples. His disciples shared both life and ministry with their master. They came alongside Him in His ministry to learn from Him by sharing in the lifestyle he modeled for them and the experiences He created for them to learn by doing. Undoubtedly, internships provide a powerful tool for sharing life and ministry with those who want to learn in the atmosphere of a mentoring experience.

The campus ministry at Eastern Illinois University has offered two types of internships. "Student internships" are offered to students who had proven themselves as top-notch student leaders in our ministry. Serving part-time, these dedicated students accepted the opportunity to get a more intense taste of what it might mean to serve as a career campus minister. However, within a very few years, it was discovered that the part-time nature of student interns stunted the benefits they could personally receive and severely limited the resources they could give to the ministry. These ended by the early 1990s.

---

[58] Another common flaw in our thinking is to equate the word, "disciple" with "apostle" and use the two very distinct terms interchangeably. But they are not interchangeable. For example, Jesus called Peter, Andrew, James and John to leave their nets and become "fishers of men." That was a call to "discipleship" and does not differ at all from any contemporary person's call to become a "Christ-follower." Later, Jesus appointed only 12 of those who had already become His disciples then to become "apostles." Cf., Luke 6:12-13, "One of those days Jesus went out to a mountainside to pray, and spent the night praying to God. When morning came, he called his disciples to him and chose twelve of them, whom he also designated apostles… ." (cf. Mark 3:13-19, NIV)

More than a decade would pass before our ministry acquired multiple staff and began to develop the internship program we currently offer. By 2005, our staff had grown and "graduate internships" were offered. We require an intern to have already received at least a bachelor's degree.[59] Our interns serve in a full-time capacity and this chapter offers practical insights on the training process. This "intern pilgrimage" offered many insights to our staff. This chapter serves to share those insights.

Interns Explore a Calling in Life

Secondly, an internship helps the graduate answer some important life questions for himself/herself. Many students graduate from excellent campus ministries. Along the way, they may have served as student leaders or small group leaders. They may have heavily invested their time, energy and money in community service or missions trips. These experiences wield the power to change the course of a student's career. Many campus ministers routinely witness large numbers of students who graduate with a university degree who, by the time they reach their senior year, passionately want to serve in vocational ministry. Not part time. Not as an avocation. Not just as an active "member" of a church; but as a chosen career. They choose to

Internships provide a unique and dynamic opportunity

[59] We did make an exception to this "graduate only" requirement for one intern. He had found that academics were not for him. However, he desperately wanted to do "blue collar" missions. He wanted to build housing for those in need. Yet, he also felt a need to have both training and experience in ministry. We honored his desire and brought him on as an intern. His huge servant's heart made him one of the most effective interns we have had.

lay aside their engineering degree, their accounting degree, their teaching degree, and embark on a search for their calling in full-time career ministry or missions. Internships provide a unique and dynamic opportunity for the graduate to test the waters—to get a taste of full-time, career ministry—to determine whether or not ministry-as-a-career is a good "fit" for them. "Am I cut out to be a campus minister?" "Do I enjoy ministry, but believe I want to serve in some other role, like children's ministry, worship ministry, or administrative ministry?" An internship holds the key for many of these young people to enable them to make this important life decision and direction. For some, the internship culminates in a career in ministry. For others, the internship will end differently. "I really enjoy serving, but I've discovered a "full-time career" in ministry just doesn't suit me." Regardless to which end an internship leads, it is still a valuable tool campus ministries can use to help graduates make these important life choices.[60]

Finding Potential Interns

Typically, interns can be found from any of three sources: 1) From within your own campus ministry; 2) From sister campus ministries; 3) From Bible colleges.

From Within Your Own Organization

In many ways, finding a graduating student in your own ministry produces the ideal scenario for intern recruitment. First of all, you will almost certainly already know the prospective intern personally. A first-hand personal knowledge of an intern candidate can prove invaluable in

[60] Since we began offering full-time graduate internships in 2005, over half of our interns have ended up in full-time ministry.

assessing whether or not the person will be a good fit. And if the candidate is someone whom you have mentored one-on-one or developed a close friendship with, you will feel much more comfortable bringing that person on as an intern simply because he/she is a known entity. You will be aware of the person's attributes and limitations—strengths and weaknesses. And you will know their depth of faith, their style of forming interpersonal relationships. Very importantly… you will have some gauge of his/her work ethic. I cannot stress strongly enough that interns need a very strong work ethic. Campus ministry requires the ability to "self start"—that is to work, vision-cast, strategize, program, study, teach, mentor, counsel, and serve without the constant reminding and prodding by a "superior" or "boss."

But, bringing someone already involved in your ministry onto your staff as an intern does bring with it some potential problems. First, the intern, having only experienced the way your particular organization operates, will not have a breadth of experience in how other ministries work. So the intern may tend to approach ministry as status quo—"same-old-same-old." Creativity may suffer.

Treat the intern as a full-fledged member of your ministry team

Second, the transition from actively involved student to a full-fledged full-time staff member can create an uncomfortable identity shift with their previous peers that feels both awkward and difficult. Most of our own ministry's interns have come from within our own organization. We have observed this transitional difficulty or awkwardness to be almost universally true for each of these "in house" interns. New interns often struggle with not feeling respected as "real ministers" by their peers.

The only way I know to help with this transition from actively involved student or student leader to full-time intern on a ministry staff is to tackle it on two fronts: 1) First, you must treat the intern as a full-fledged member of your ministry team (not as a junior partner, and definitely not as a mere "gopher.") Second, you must present the intern to the students in your ministry as such. This is the approach we have taken. When an intern is accepted and signs a contract with our ministry, I make it very clear that from day one of their internship they automatically become equal partners in ministry with the rest of our career staff. To bring that point home, interns are included in virtually every facet of staff decision making. In fact, since we have 4 full-time career staff, if we have three interns… those three interns and one career staff member can vote down almost any idea, plan, or project that I bring up as senior campus minister. And I have grown to be completely comfortable with that.[61]

Recruiting from Other Campus Ministries

Sister campus ministries can provide a rich resource pool for potential interns for your ministry. We have acquired fifteen percent of our past interns from other ministries similar to ours. All of these ministries were out of state.

Great benefits for you and your organization can inure by hiring an intern from outside your own ministry. The intern will have grown up in a different college and ministry culture from your own. As such, the intern can serve as a rich,

[61] Of course, if the issue at hand were something pertaining to a shift in foundational doctrine for our ministry, or something possibly illegal or against university policy, I chose to step in and negate the vote. That is a role that our board of directors expects me to assume in my role as senior campus minister.

creative resource for fresh ideas he/she can implement in your ministry.

Dangers do exist, though. Most stem from the unknown. You don't know this person, nor does the person know you. Because of this, the intern may struggle with feeling like an "outsider." Outside interns don't know the students in your ministry. They don't know you. So their first obstacle may emerge from the struggle to feel like they belong. You may need to help them find a circle of friends within your ministry who can take them under their wings, socially. These interns may also struggle with your structure and methodologies. Making the transition from the way their previous campus ministry operated will likely contrast with the way yours operates. You may find that these interns will often say, "Well, in my campus ministry at the school I attended, we didn't do it that way." Two of our outside interns struggled significantly trying to understand the philosophical reasons behind our structure—which differed pretty radically from their experience in the campus ministry in which they grew up as students. You will need to assume nothing and work diligently to teach, train, and constantly explain why your organization does ministry in the way it does. All the while, respecting these intern's backgrounds and experiences which may differ from those of the culture of your campus ministry.

If you pursue interns from outside your own ministry, check personal references with a fine-toothed comb. Knowing the campus ministry staff at the sister ministry, and knowing them well, is crucial in this selection process. You need references for potential interns from co-workers you personally know well enough that you can trust their judgment and their iron-clad guarantee that they are giving you an open and honest assessment of the candidate. Seek out references from both the candidate's ministry team as well as his/her peers (fellow students and roommates), and even former professors. Each of these reference sources can help you know the candidate better.

Recruiting from Bible Colleges

Ambiguity. Ambiguity hung like a dark cloud over my investigation into the practical wisdom and the practical experiences gleaned from my peers in campus ministry as I polled them about recruiting interns from Bible colleges. Perennially our staff receives requests from Bible college students (not graduates) who desire to do their school-mandated internship with us. The problem has been that their college requires a one-semester internship, and we will not entertain bringing on an intern for less than a full year. Legwork for writing this chapter included polling as many of my peers in campus ministry as possible regarding their experiences bringing Bible college students onto their staff as interns.

The results of this poll were very mixed. Ambiguous. One of those campus ministers polled indicated that he had employed three interns. Two were Bible college students who served for one semester. The third came from another campus ministry. He appreciated the Bible college interns' knowledge of Scripture. And he appreciated that neither of them "…had any preconceived notions about campus ministry." The intern he recruited from another campus ministry seemed to focus on "this is how we did it at … ." So this campus minister saw benefits and challenges in both choices. He did, however, adamantly express that one semester is not enough time. By the time the one semester passed the Bible college interns "…were just getting settled in when it was time to go."

Another risk with hiring Bible college interns (or full-time staff, for that matter) arises from two questions: 1) Has this Bible college student ever had any involvement with a university campus ministry? And, 2) What preconceptions, biases, and opinions does the Bible college student hold toward the university experience and university students? I have encountered many Bible college students who love university life and university students. They do not view Christians who attend the university as "second class citizens in the Kingdom." However, on a few other occasions, I have encountered Bible college students who maintain a personal air of spiritual superiority and a judgmental attitude toward both the university and their brothers and sisters who attend one. Again, from my poll, another close friend in campus ministry who has employed interns and staff from both Bible college and university backgrounds weighed in on his experience with Bible college interns: *"I approach Bible college applicants with a great deal of caution—especially those who have not had any experience with campus ministry or a university campus. What I think is important to figure out about them is their 'posture' toward the university and toward students who aren't from church or Christian backgrounds. Are they able to connect with students and culture that is outside of the Christian bubble?"*

Interns from Bible Colleges can certainly do well

An inherent irony rears its ugly head in this controversy. The majority of long-term, veteran campus ministers—those who began in the 1970s and 1980s—came on the campus with a Bible college education. We learned the strengths and weaknesses of our background. Yet many came from a background that included both a university and a Bible college education experience. This brings the most wide-ranging experience to the campus ministry.

Interns from Bible colleges can certainly do well. Those who also attended a university will likely understand both secular university students and the culture of the campus ministry better. Dismissing Bible college prospects for internships, generally speaking, is not a wise choice. But you must exercise due diligence to insure that the Bible college prospect will adequately fit into the role.

Application Process and Interview

Hiring an intern without a detailed and thorough application and interview process increases the likelihood of failure. Do not enter into this process naïvely. Just because you know the prospective intern well, you must shoulder your responsibility to process the candidate through an application and interview process. And in a multiple staff ministry, every staff member should be involved in this process.[62] Depending on your specific situation, your board of directors may also want to be involved. In our case, hiring career ministry staff falls under the purview of our board. But our board has delegated hiring interns completely to our career staff.[63]

[62] I can, however envision ministries for which this would not be practical. For a campus ministry with 20-30 full-time staff members having every staff member involved in this process would prove to be clumsy. I would assume, though, that ministries that large would already have their own internship program well in hand. So, I feel that I am not really writing to meet their needs, but the needs of those who may not have initiated an internship program, or who have, but have not experienced rewarding results.

[63] Our staff very deeply appreciates our board's trust in us to make wise decisions about interns. Delegating this responsibility to staff also frees the board from one more tedious task.

The Application

Most people probably view an application as a one-way document, i.e., you are saying to the prospective intern, "Tell me about yourself." But a more useful application begins by offering the applicant information he/she needs to determine if they even want or need to fill it out and turn it in—and that can save both you and the prospective intern time wasted.

What Should the Application Tell the Prospective Intern?

A well thought out application accomplishes at least ten informational purposes:

1) It informs the applicant who your ministry is.

2) It spells out the purpose(s) of the internship.

3) It offers a general summary of what the intern's job entails.

4) It quantifies the qualifications for acceptance.

5) It lists the goals and objectives the staff intends for the intern experience to achieve.

6) It spells out accountability, i.e., to whom does the intern report?

7) It lists the general responsibilities of an intern and then the specific job expectations (or specifies how the intern's job description will be determined).

8) It should specify the exact dates for the time frame of the intern's employment.

9) It should cover some of the policies regarding finances, such as: Can the intern also have an outside job? What "business expenses" (travel, supplies, books, etc.) are covered by the ministry's budget?

10) Finally, it should state what salary the intern will be earning. This salary statement should also spell out the ministry's expectations for fundraising—especially if the intern is required to raise all or part of their own salary and expenses; and it also should spell out the process from application through interview, the deadline for the staff to either accept or deny the application, and finally, a deadline for the intern to notify the staff whether they accept or decline the offer of an intern position. This is all a part of an introduction to the actual application.

What Should the Application Ask From the Prospective Intern?

Find out basic information from the applicant: name, current address, hometown, home church, phone number, email address, degree/major and date of completion along with GPA. The application should also include several questions to be answered in mini-essay form. Here are some examples:

1. What (if any) are your future ministry goals or aspirations?
2. What is it about campus ministry (or this specific ministry) that excites or draws you?
3. What do you feel that you can contribute to this ministry? (Do not limit your answer to only those activities that you have already seen the current staff or interns perform—feel free to "think outside the box").
4. What fears/concerns do you have regarding serving as an intern?
5. What other options are you considering post-graduation (e.g., graduate school, job, etc.)?
6. What do you personally hope to gain from this

internship?

7. How do you feel about raising 100% of your own financial support?

8. Are you currently in a dating relationship? How would this relationship (or not being in a relationship) impact your internship?

9. In our ministry, we teach that being a Christian means having a personal relationship with God. We teach that a person enters into that relationship by the following means: *hearing* the gospel message (John 6:45, Romans 10:17), *believing/having faith* in Jesus (John 5:24, Mark 16:16, John 1:12), *confessing* Jesus as Lord (Romans 10:9, Matthew 10:32-33), *repenting* of sin (Acts 2:38, Acts 17:30), and *being baptized* (immersed in water) (Acts 2:38, Romans 6:3-4, Acts 10:48). As Christians, we are called to a life of discipleship which is characterized by obedience to God's Word. Do you agree or disagree with this teaching? Explain.

10. List your perceived areas of spiritual giftedness, natural talents, skills, and/or interests.

11. Provide a list of references with contact information for each one.

The Interview

If you work in a multiple staff ministry, you will probably find it very beneficial to meet just before the interview to discuss all of the positives and any concerns each staff member can share about their own personal assessment of the prospect's application. Our staff begins an interview by asking the applicant to perform a self-evaluation, reflecting on some of the very same questions already answered on the application. We have found that allowing the prospect to respond verbally often helps clear up questions or concerns we might have had from the answers on the application.

Time Frame for Effective Internships

I have already hinted at this, but anything less than a year will severely limit the success of the internship for both the intern and your ministry. In the poll I took among my peers in campus ministry this rang as a constant and consistent theme. It takes a semester just to acclimate to the role (even longer if you have hired an intern not from your ministry). By the second semester, the intern can reassess his/her experience based on the first semester, perform mid-course corrections, and maximize the remaining time in service. We require one year, with the option to offer the intern a second year if we feel it will be mutually beneficial. We also have become convinced that the ideal start time is just before the Association of Campus Ministries' annual Campus Ministers' Retreat (CMR). We require new interns to attend CMR (normally in late May or early June) with the spoken expectation that they will intentionally interact with other campus ministers and return energized and motivated. This start time also allows a new intern to use the entire summer to acclimate to the job and begin to accomplish some of our "curriculum" requirements before the hectic fall semester kicks off.

Jesus spent time with his disciples individually and in groups

The Training Component

WWJD? What would Jesus do? Really???!!! Pardon this clichéd "blast from the past," but when it came to His disciples, we know one thing for sure: He spent time with them individually and in groups; and He taught them HOW to be His disciples both by what He said and by what He did. We also know that He placed expectations on them and gave them tasks to perform.[64] Here are some ways we follow Jesus' model:

Interns Need to be Mentored

They need a regular time set aside to meet with a staff mentor. Mentoring an intern requires mutual transparency. It requires that the mentor have the courage to hold the intern accountable for his/her personal spiritual life, relationships, and ongoing ministry responsibilities. A mentor sometimes needs to ask hard questions about these categories in the intern's life. But the mentor also needs to offer encouragement and recognition of the intern's faithful and successful performance.

---

[64] Two examples of Jesus' tasking his disciples in a hands-on learning environment: First, In Luke 9:1-10 we find the record of Jesus' first training mission for the 12. He sent them out *"...to proclaim the kingdom of God and to perform healing."* On this training mission they were cautioned by Jesus to *"Take nothing for your journey, neither a staff, nor a bag, nor bread, nor money; and do not even have two tunics apiece. Whatever house you enter, stay there until you leave that city."* Jesus expected these men to live by faith, relying solely on God's provision through people.

Second, then, in Luke 10:1-24, Jesus sent out a group of 70 disciples on a similar mission and with similar restrictions for their own daily care and sustenance.

Curriculum

A successful internship program needs a well thought out curriculum geared to offer the intern a knowledge base for ministry. A well-balanced curriculum includes training modules, a reading program, and writing assignments.

Curriculum: Training Modules

Bless your interns by providing them quality, structured, well-prepared and purposeful training modules. Without structured training, the intern will labor devoid of the knowledge base necessary to perform at peak proficiency. Here is a suggested list of training modules that can provide a balanced, knowledge-based diet for your intern(s).

1. Discovering Your Spiritual Gifts and Ministry Passion – The DISC tool
2. Preparing and Delivering Large Group Teachings
3. Counseling—Basic Skills
4. Worship (Personal and Corporate)
5. Computer Skills Development
6. Missions Trips—Planning and Execution
7. Small Group Bible Study Administration
8. Support Raising and Follow-Up
9. Mentoring students
10. Budgeting, How and Why
11. Time Management

The DISC[65] is a tool that we have found to be extremely beneficial, not just for interns, but for our entire

---

[65] The DISC is an acronym for Discover Your Giftedness, by Mels Carbonell PhD. Uniquely You™ Resources; P O Box 490 Blue Ridge, GA 30513. (800) 501-0490. Website: www.myuy.com. Email:

staff. The DISC workbook identifies both a person's Spiritual Gifts and "personality type." It ranks their Spiritual Gifts from strongest to weakest; it also not only identifies an individual's "personality type," but via several charts shows how the person's unique personality type might affect the way in which they best utilize their Spiritual Gifts. We actually begin our intern's first week on the job by going through each staff members' and each interns' DISC results in a small group/staff meeting setting. This all-day exercise has proven invaluable in helping us to understand ourselves and one another better, and to understand what strengths and weaknesses we might possess both individually and as a team.[66]

Curriculum: Reading Program

A structured reading program is crucial to the development of the intern as an effective minister and as a whole person. By "structured" I mean that the ministry staff needs to come up with a plan for the intern's reading, and part of that plan needs to be to intentionally omit any lightweight or shallow

We respect a strong comprehensive work ethic in ministry

drmels@myuy.com. This tool comes in several variations, depending mostly on the number of Spiritual Gifts the tool inventories and identifies. We have found the 9 Spiritual Gift version to be ideal. The DISC is not inexpensive, but can be bought in bulk at a discount.

[66] Each individual will need their own copy of the DISC. It is designed and copyrighted for single use only. And it cannot be photocopied—either legally or practically, since the question/answer assessment portion is printed on carbonless transfer copy paper. Fortunately, once your staff has taken the DISC, they will not need to do it again, so it is a one-time expense. However, it is a tool that you might want to take again every 5-10 years. We have found that the longer you are in ministry the more some key aspects of your life change.

reading material. The poor reading habits of all too many college and graduate students is discouraging. Interns may find the reading requirements to be the most challenging part of their time spent as an intern. But they must become overwhelming convinced that reading good books does not end merely as a syllabus item in the college classroom. Ministers must read to self-feed and find challenges from sources smarter or more experienced in broad arenas of knowledge outside their own life collection of knowledge.

A couple of years ago my wife, Sue, and I visited one of our supporting churches for their Sunday morning worship service. Their church attendance enjoys a healthy growth mode, moving from about 600 then and now approaching 1000. In the middle of his sermon, the senior minister proclaimed, "I hate reading, so I never read. I can't remember the last time I read a book." As we drove home, Sue and I couldn't help but talk about his blatant admission. The shallowness of his preaching seemed evident. Now we knew, at least in part, why. That may sound harsh, but we respect a strong, comprehensive work ethic in ministry. Refusing to broaden your intellectual horizons and deepen your spiritual roots by shunning reading does not make for a good work ethic in ministry. If you do not eat, you will not have the strength to feed others. You will wither, starve, and die.

The interns' reading program should require each intern to read eight books during their internship. Purchase the books for them. Let them keep them. Provide a select bibliography of 50-100 books for them to choose from. Categorize the books under major themes, such as apologetics, evangelism, missions, counseling, theology, Christian living, discipleship, leadership, campus ministry, and mentoring. Allow interns to choose four to six books from that list as "electives." Then involve the staff to discuss the top two to four books each intern must read.[67] Require a brief, one-page "reflection paper"—not a book report, and not a critique, but a personal statement of what they "took away" from their reading. If your interns begin at the start of summer, they can use that slower-paced time in your ministry to hit the reading hard.

Curriculum: Writing Program

The intern will gain tremendous blessings by engaging in few writing assignments, such as:

Journaling

The intern will find enormous strength and confidence by keeping a journal during the internship. The journal, containing personal observations and perceptions about his/her experiences and spiritual journey, becomes a

[67] Currently, we require these four books: 1) **Knowing God**, by J.I. Packer. If I were to require only one book this would be it. Packer's book is a contemporary classic. It is not an easy read—especially since I encourage the intern to look up every Biblical reference Packer lists. There is some influence of Reformed Theology, but you can mentor the intern in those areas. 2) **The Universe Next Door**, by James Sire. This eye-opening book will acquaint the intern with the major world views. It is an indispensable resource for getting Christians to open their minds and step inside the shoes of non-Christian people. 3) **Church History in Plain Language**, by Bruce L. Shelley. This easy read is lengthy, but can help the intern gain a grasp of the successes and failures repeated throughout the history of the Church. And 4) **Union in Truth**, by James B. North. An excellent history of the Restoration Movement. Many interns will have come from a variety of denominational backgrounds and this book will acquaint them with the genius of this movement which stressed Christian unity, Biblical authority, and non-denominational discipleship. Note: This book is currently out of print, but new and used copies are readily available from online sellers such as Amazon.com and Ebay. Due to its out of print status, this is the one book that we purchase and only loan to the interns to read.

logbook of their growth and challenges in ministry. Entries should be made at least each week (but can be made daily). The journal should be confidential. Staff should not read it. But the intern should be encouraged to share with their staff-mentor any insights, questions, or concerns arising from the journaling experience. For accountability, ask the intern to report on their journaling each week (perhaps at each regular staff meeting). They will report only on their completion or non-completion of the task for that week. If you want them to journal openly and honestly, do not require them to report details of what they have written.

Personal Vision Statement

One of the first projects the intern should produce is a one-to-three page paper encapsulating their own personal vision for their internship. In the vision statement, the intern should be encouraged to address the following themes:

a) Vision: For example… "What do I want to do/accomplish this year? What specific things do I want to see happen during my internship? What aspects of ministry will I attempt? In what specific areas do I see myself serving?

b) Purpose: Address the "Why?" of your internship in terms of the vision you have cast for your year.

c) Goals: What specific tasks, ministries, or programs do you want to accomplish, and how will you go about achieving those specific goals?

d) Tools for Measuring progress. In other words, "How will you measure or assess whether or not your goals have been achieved and your purpose has been realized?"

The intern should actually write two vision statements. The first should be completed within the first five weeks of employment so that the interns can begin to work at fulfilling the tasks they have taken on as their primary thrust in ministry. The second should be completed early in the second semester. This second paper can be almost identical to the first if nothing has changed. However, most interns will find that some of their initial ideas either did not work, were too much to bite off, or the students showed no interest. And often the intern will have grown sufficiently during the first semester of experience that they have outgrown the original vision and want to expand.

Three Theology of Ministry Papers

Who is God? Who is Jesus? Who is the Holy Spirit? What is the Gospel message?, etc. (5-8 pages in length, and due prior to the end of the first 1/3 of the internship. You will need to set the appropriate date.)

Discipleship:

What characterizes a growing relationship with God? What does it mean to follow Jesus? What part do spiritual disciplines play in the believer's relationship with God?, etc. (3-5 pages in length, and due before the end of the second 1/3 of the internship. You will need to set the appropriate date.)

Ministry:

What would a Biblically functioning church look like? What is the role of a minister in the church? What is the role of the members? How can my giftedness and passion be used to further God's purposes? (3-5 pages in length. Due prior to the end of the last 1/3 of the internship. You will need to set the appropriate date).

A Summary or Exit Paper:

The Interns should complete a 3-4-page paper at the end of their internship reflecting on their experience as well as assessing the experience. This paper should be due at least one to two weeks prior to the intern's departure from their employment.

The Importance of Evaluations

Each intern should be evaluated informally by their assigned staff mentor throughout the internship and formally by the entire staff at the end of each semester. The evaluation could be based on:

- How well the intern has accomplished their targets outlined in their "Vision Statement"
- Active and willing participation in the ministry activities.
- Effectiveness in areas of assigned or accepted responsibility.
- Completion of reading and written assignments.
- Overall performance.

The evaluation should be performed in an atmosphere of love and encouragement. The purpose of the evaluation is to help, not chastise the intern.

Consider Dating Relationships with Interns

Setting specific guidelines for the interns dating life is a good idea. Will interns be allowed to date members of the ministry? If so, under what conditions? Will the intern be required to consult their staff mentor before initiating an in-ministry dating relationship? How about a dating relationship with someone outside the ministry? As you consider this tough subject, your goal should not be to control the intern, but to assure that a godly dating relationship is being modeled.

It's a "Kingdom thing"

Taking on interns is NOT to be done selfishly. Hiring interns to do menial tasks is insulting. Taking on interns just so that our own ministry personally benefits is prideful. Internships truly represent an unselfish Kingdom-focused gift to Jesus. The overarching goal of enlisting, enabling, and empowering interns is to make dynamic, servant-hearted disciples who can go into the world and bless churches, missions, and other ministries with the knowledge, tools, and experience they gleaned by spending time with us in this unique role - intern.

To God be the glory.

Roger Songer, originally from Newton, Illinois, studied engineering at Rose Hulman Institute of Technology. He attended St. Louis Christian College and Lincoln Christian College and Trinity Evangelical Divinity School. He served as campus minister for 38 years. Roger married his high school sweetheart, Sue, in 1974. They have three grown daughters, Rachel, Leah, and Rebekah. They have been blessed with six grandchildren.

Chapter 11

GLOBAL INFLUENCE AT ARM'S REACH

By Barry Reed

When Jesus stood in front of His followers before his ascension, he told them, *"Go, and make disciples of all the nations, baptizing them in the name of the Father, and of the Son and of the Holy Spirit. And teaching them to obey all I have commanded you. And surely I am with you always to the very end of the age."*[68] This commission on Jesus' first followers motivated them to take any avenue necessary to communicate that salvation is only found in a commitment to Jesus Christ. Today, as people from many nations have heard and accepted this message, many others have either heard and rejected it, not heard it or grown hostile to it.

To understand the language of this command is important for a disciple to see the world and the mission to make disciples of all the nations holistically. So often a conversation about the Great Commission gets focused predominately on sending Christ-followers to other unreached or under-reached world nations. Not that this is a wrong practice, but the text appears to be more than this after further study on the words recorded. "The word *nations* here is a translation of *ethne,* meaning ethnic groups rather than geographical states as we understand them today. *Ethnos* is a defined group of people who have a common culture and

---

[68] *The Holy Bible: New International Version*, (Grand Rapids, MI: Zondervan, 1984) Matthew 28:19-20.

ancestry binding them together in such a way as to give them a distinct identity. This identity is expressed in their worldview, common values, beliefs and behaviors."[69] No doubt, a follower of Jesus must go to unreached people with the gospel, as Jesus commands his followers, but by no means does that specify that the going part must be across geographical borders. So in a country like America where different ethnic groups are regularly coming into the country and crossing with other ethnic groups, the opportunity to "go and make disciples of all the nations," is much closer than it might first appear.

> *The opportunity to go and make disciples of all nations is much closer than it might first appear*

What is more interesting than just the large amount of people immigrating to the United States is where these people are coming from. It might seem obvious that the primary country new US residents are immigrating from is Mexico. But what might not be so obvious is the second, third and fourth largest immigrating countries are China, India and the Philippines.[70] In fact, in 2012, China and India's combined immigrating population to the U.S. was more than Mexico's immigrating population. Considering these three countries are under evangelized, harder to mobilize the Church in, and in some respects, hostile toward the Christian witness, the Church of America ought to be excited about the opportunity

---

[69] David Boyd, *You Don't have to Cross the Ocean to Reach the World: The Power of Local Cross-Cultural Ministry* (Grand Rapids, MI: Baker Books, 2008), 26.

[70] Department of Homeland Security, *Persons Obtaining Legal Permanent Resident Status by Region and Country of Birth: Fiscal Years 2003 to 2012*, (accessed January 31, 2014), http://www.dhs.gov/yearbook-immigration-statistics-2012-legal-permanent-residents.

coming to her doorsteps and screaming, "The nations are coming!"[71]

During the 2012-2013 school year, American colleges and universities were home to 819,644 international college students.[72] The international student population has increased almost every year in thc United States since the late 1940, with only four years in exception. In addition, approximately two-thirds of these international students came from countries identified in the 10/40 Window. 10/40 Window countries exist from the northwestern countries of Africa, east through southern Asia to Indonesia. [73] In this region of the world live the majority of unreached people groups with the gospel of Jesus. These people being mostly unreached, "is due to a combination of geographic, linguistic, political, religious, social and spiritual barriers."[74] With such a high number of college students coming to America from such countries, the Church in America should be raising awareness and calling for action, as the opportunity to reach the unreached nations with the gospel is coming increasingly more within reach every year.

Why focus on international students more than the average international person coming to the United States? Impact Campus Ministries says, "If you impact the U (university), you impact the World." This slogan phrase

---

[71] Jason Mandryk, editor, *Operation World: The Definitive Prayer Guide to Every Nation, 7th ed.* (Downers Grove: InterVarsity Press, 2012) 228-251, 418-446.

[72] "Open Doors 2013 Fast Facts," Institute of International Education, http://www.iie.org/Research-and-Publications/Open-Doors/Data/International-Students/Enrollment-Trends/1948-2012, (accessed November 22, 2013).

[73] "What is the 10/40 Window?," The Joshua Project, http://www.joshuaproject.net/10-40-window.php (accessed December 13, 2013).

[74] Jason Mandryk, editor, *Operation World: The Definitive Prayer Guide to Every Nation, 7th ed.* (Downers Grove: InterVarsity Press, 2012) 25.

simply means that a dominant number of world influencers attend college in the United States of America. If disciples of Jesus can find a way to make disciples of international students, eventually, many of those students of today will be the world leaders of tomorrow. What if those future world leaders were not only trained at their university academically, but were transformed by the power of the Holy Spirit before they returned home? The Washington Times reported in 2012 that the US State Department listed nearly 300 world leaders who all received higher education in the United States before they assumed their position of power.[75] Well known and highly respected international student minister, Dr. Robert Taussig worked with thousands of international students at Kansas State University in Manhattan, Kansas. He would tell audiences when he spoke, "If history repeats itself, fifty percent of the world's future presidents are studying on American college campuses right now."[76] From Church history, we know that from the days Jesus walked the earth, the Roman Empire was hostile toward the Christian movement. Eventually, through the disciples of Jesus making disciples of the nations, the Roman leadership became disciples of Jesus, landmarked by Emperor Constantine, a Christian convert, issuing the Edict of Milan, making Christianity a legal religion.[77] Could the

Nearly 300 world leaders received their education in the United States before they assumed their position of power

[75] Ben Wolfgang, "Armed with U.S. education, many leaders take on world," The Washington Times:August 19, 2012, http://www.washingtontimes.com/news/2012/aug/19/armed-with-us-education-many-leaders-take-on-world (accessed December 14, 2013).
[76] Told to Greg Swinney of Crossroads International Student Ministries, March 2010.
[77] Edward Gibbon, *The History of the Decline and Fall of the Roman Empire* (New York: Fred De Fau and Co. Publishers, 1906) 219.

university campus be the road to transforming other earthly nations with God fearing leaders at the top, much like happened in Rome?

When Jesus called His followers to make disciples, His instruction to go was not so much an instruction of directional movement but directional purpose. Being a disciple of Jesus meant living life in a risky way, rather than hiding, because life had a directional purpose. Wherever disciples of Jesus go, and wherever there are ones who need to hear about Jesus, those disciples are expected to share the message of Christ. A significant resource the American Church has available is campus ministries already established and working with college students on campuses across the country. Most campus ministries are registered student clubs or organizations, giving those groups of Christians special access to all students who attend the campus on which they minister, including international students.

What if these campus ministries were all aware of the opportunity before them as God leads future leaders from 10/40 Window countries to their campuses? What if those campus ministries were equipped and mobilized to intentionally connect with and witness to these unreached students? What if these international students from unreached nations return home not only with a degree in higher education, but also with a testimony of how Jesus saved their lives? What if campus ministries were leading domestic and international Christian students, along with local churches to participate in this wonderful blessing God has granted to reach the unreached nations as they come to us? With such an opportunity before the American church, how can a campus ministry leader lead others to intentionally minister to the unreached nations among them? Beginning with biblical motivation and cultural understanding, campus ministry leaders can teach and mobilize disciples of Jesus to build relationships, plant seeds of the Gospel and seek to make disciples of the least reached nations attending American colleges and universities.

Domestic Student Ministry to International Students

Campus ministries are primarily populated by domestic students of which a campus ministry can train and mobilize to reach international students. Leading domestic students to be active in ministering to international students is not an easy task. Campus ministry leaders from campuses like University of Illinois express frustration trying to motivate domestic students to connect with international students. The University of Illinois has the second largest international student population in America,[78] so the population is easily visible on campus. Why is it difficult to motivate domestic students to minister to them? The domestic students at the University of Illinois are like the rest of Americans. Multicultural interaction in America is difficult. In most parts of this country, people socialize and live among people who are just like themselves. The Church in America has similar tendencies.

Christians in America identify a whole lot more with a negative characteristic of the biblical Jonah than they would like to admit. When Jonah was called by God to preach to foreigners rather than Israel, Jonah ran from bringing the news of God's Kingdom to the people of Nineveh. The attitude of Jonah parallels with the core attitude of many

[78] Open Doors 2013 Fast Facts from www.iie.org reveal University of Illinois at Urbana-Champaign having the second largest international student population at 9,804 students. This data can be located at http://www.iie.org/Research-and-Publications/Open-Doors.

American Christians when talking about international relationships and interactions. Jonah was fine with carrying out his prophetic duties amongst the Israelites, but by no means did he want to associate with the pagan people of Nineveh. However, the people of Nineveh were made in the image of God just as the Israelites, so they also mattered to God.[79] The same is true today. All people, from all ethnic groups, matter to God, even people from Muslim, Buddhist, and Hindu territory are worthy of hearing the Gospel of Jesus, just like those from Christian territory.

In my hometown of Macomb, IL there is a Korean Christian Fellowship, a Redeemed Christian Fellowship which is specifically for African immigrants and students, and other churches that do not carry a specific people group label yet only specific people groups attend. So, how does a campus ministry help domestic Christian students venture beyond the comfort of ministering to only domestic students when the church culture they grew up in was most likely only reaching out to one ethnic group? I am convinced, as well as many other campus ministers, that Christian leaders must begin with biblical teaching about evangelism to all nations for the Kingdom of God.[80] After presenting domestic students with a solid knowledge of God's desire for reaching all ethnic groups, a leader will need to help students experience interaction with other ethnic groups to build empathy. Then domestic students can be mobilized in a variety of ways to begin building relational bridges with other ethnic groups for seeds of the gospel to be planted in their lives.

---

[79] Ralph Winter and Steven Hawthorne, editors, *Perspectives on the World Christian Movement, 3rd edition*, (Carlisle, United Kingdom: Paternoster Publishing, 1999), 30.

[80] All international student ministers listed in the bibliography, agree with this assessment.

Biblical Teaching on Evangelism for Domestic Students

"Most of us do not welcome diversity into our lives. It forces us to change, disrupts our cozy patterns, engages us in a world where our deficiencies are exposed."[81] However, Christ has not called the Church to cling to our individualism. Christ has called us to be witnesses to the nations, meaning all ethnic groups. This call to the Church is not an isolated account in scripture as there are many powerful stories and commandments a Christian leader can point domestic students toward to help them see God's vision for evangelism.

Created in the Image of God

Genesis 1:26-27:

26 *Then God said, "Let us make man in our image, in our*
likeness, and let them rule over the fish of the sea and the
birds of the air, over the livestock, over all the earth, and over
all the creatures that move along the ground."
27 *So God created man in his own image, in the image of God*
he created him; male and female he created them.[82]

Just as William Wilberforce sparked the liberation of slaves by helping the citizens of Britain in the late 1700's understand that all people, of every race, are equally valuable, created in the image of God, so can a Christian leader today stress this same truth to motivate change for evangelism. All human beings, from every country in the world, are created in the image of God,

Christ has called us to be witnesses to the nations, that means all ethnic groups

[81] Duane Elmer, *Cross-Cultural Conflict: Building Relationships for Effective Ministry*, (Downers Grove, IL: InterVarsity Press, 1993), 23.
[82] *The Holy Bible: New International Version*, (Grand Rapids, MI: Zondervan, 1984) Genesis 1:26-27.

and therefore matter to God. If all human beings matter to God, then all human beings should matter to Christians.[83] To lead a domestic student to consider the Kingdom of God as greater than people just like them, this basic biblical teaching is foundational. With this foundation, a leader can more easily have a conversation about the action Jesus calls for to all ethnic groups in the Great Commission of Matthew 28:19-20.

A Blessing to All People

In Genesis 12, God appears to Abraham and promises to make his family into a great nation and all people on earth would be blessed through Abraham's family.[84] Later passages from the New Testament (i.e. Galatians 3:26-29 & Ephesians 2:1-3:6) communicate that the Church is the fruit of this promise to Abraham. The Church is the hands and feet of Jesus Christ on earth. It is also through Abraham's family that God sent salvation through Jesus Christ. And following Jesus commissioning His followers to make disciples, it is still through Abraham's family that God is doing redemptive work and communicating the salvation message.[85] With over 200,000 international students coming to American universities from China alone, the opportunity to be part of the blessing that connects people with the resurrected Jesus for the first time greatly exists on a college campus.[86]

---

[83] Michael Pocock & Joseph Henriques, *Cultural Change & Your Church: Helping Your Church Thrive in a Diverse Society*, (Grand Rapids, Michigan: Baker Books, 2002), 84.
[84] Ralph Winter and Steven Hawthorne, editors, *Perspectives on the World Christian Movement, 3rd edition*, (Carlisle, United Kingdom: Paternoster Publishing, 1999), 3.
[85] Michael Pocock & Joseph Henriques, *Cultural Change & Your Church: Helping Your Church Thrive in a Diverse Society*, (Grand Rapids, Michigan: Baker Books, 2002), 89.
[86] 2013 Open Doors Data from www.iie.org – During the 2012-2013 school year 235,597 college students from China were studying in the USA. This was an increase of over 40,000 Chinese students from the previous school

Responsibility Toward Aliens

For many international students, their arrival in America is a first-time experience. Understandably, they feel lost and afraid, and it takes a while to get comfortable with their new surroundings. Even at the point that they get more comfortable with their surroundings and daily routine, most still feel like an outsider. In Leviticus 19:33-34 God reminds his people that they have a responsibility to the aliens who live among them.

[33] *"When an alien lives with you in your land, do not mistreat him.* [34] *The alien living with you must be treated as one of your native-born. Love him as yourself, for you were aliens in Egypt. I am the LORD your God.* [87]

The whole nation of Israel lived in Egypt for hundreds of years and after God rescued them and led them out of Egypt and to the Promise Land, He reminded them that as they were once foreigners, they should continue to love the foreigners who are among them.[88] Though most all domestic students have never lived as a foreigner in a strange land, the principle and call to God's people still exist, that the Church is to treat foreign-born people in the same way they treat those from their home. This does not just mean we provide for their needs and give them the same human rights, but also it means we see them as valuable for the Kingdom of God as well.

---

year. This data can be located at http://www.iie.org/Research-and-Publications/Open-Doors.

[87] *The Holy Bible: New International Version*, (Grand Rapids, MI: Zondervan, 1984), Leviticus 19:33–34.

[88] Michael Pocock & Joseph Henriques, *Cultural Change & Your Church: Helping Your Church Thrive in a Diverse Society*, (Grand Rapids, Michigan: Baker Books, 2002) 38.

Focused on the Mountain Top

College is a time when most people begin making most of their daily decision for themselves. In their transition from the structure of the home they grew up in, to living apart from the family, even Christian domestic students can struggle with priorities and the temptations that lurk around each day. In a similar way, when God rescued the nation of Israel from Egypt, they too were figuring out how to live and make decisions without the routine structure placed on them while in Egypt. In Exodus 20, we read that God gave these newly liberated people ten basic commands for life under his authority. The first of which is the most important:

College students have versions of the golden calf pressuring them

Exodus 20:2-3:

2 *"I am the LORD your God, who brought you out of Egypt, out of the land of slavery.* 3 *"You shall have no other gods before me."*[89]

After Moses delivered all the instructions of God to the Israelite people, God called Moses back up to the top of the mountain to receive the written Law on stone tablets. In Exodus 32, Moses is still meeting with God up on the mountain, and the Israelites at the bottom of the mountain get distracted from the first command; God being their only God. In their fear and uncertainty, the people crafted a golden calf out of the precious metals they possessed and decide to worship this golden calf that they made as their god, rather

[89] *The Holy Bible: New International Version*, (Grand Rapids, MI: Zondervan, 1984), Exodus 20:2–3.

than keeping focused on the true God who was meeting with Moses up on the mountain.

College students have versions of the golden calf pressuring them to turn their primary focus away from God and to something less than worthy every day. Predominant golden calf-like distractions include degree programs, social life and relationships. From faculty members, parents, and class-mates, a college student will constantly be fed encouragement, deadlines, grades and stories of academic failure, pressuring them to remain focused on their degree program. The danger for many is, this pressure can turn a student into one that makes their degree program the only priority, and everything else in life must wait until the degree program is complete. For many Christian students, their external pressures convince them that their relationship with God is also something that should wait until after college. A Christian student giving into this temptation makes them ineffective and unproductive for the Gospel during an important time in their life when the ethnic groups of the world are so close.

Living the "college-life" or experiencing the "social scene" of a college campus is another distracting and even sometimes dangerous golden calf-like distraction. Additionally, college students seem to have an added pressure to find their spouse before leaving college. As a result, extra time outside of the classroom not dedicated to homework, is invested in only personal gratification resulting in another person becoming a golden calf.

No matter what it is, whatever a Christian would put in place of their priority to God is just another golden calf that they dance around like the children of Israel did in Exodus 32. A degree program, social life and relationships are not unimportant, but should not become the first place of allegiance in a Christian student's life, but be subject to their first allegiance to God. This being the case, a domestic Christian student can be reminded to keep priorities straight under the authority of God, with their eyes focused on the mountain top where God is, rather than keeping focused on all the golden calf-like things at the base of the mountain. If a Christian student is keeping focused on their priority to worship God only, they should have room in their schedule to be focused on Great Commission activities and invest in the different ethnic groups that surround them every day.

Send Them on Their Way Rejoicing in God

In Acts 8, Phillip is called by God to minister to an Ethiopian. In the beginning of the chapter, Phillip is participating in a great working of the Holy Spirit in Samaria. From this event, Phillip is called away by God to go down the road that runs from Jerusalem to Gaza. Phillip was not in Jerusalem specifically, but he was still in his home country of Israel. On this road he encounters a man from Ethiopia. God tells Phillip to go to the man and, when he does, he hears him reading from Isaiah. After a conversation about what the man was reading, Phillip tells the man about Jesus Christ. Eventually, Phillip baptizes the man, and after the Holy Spirit leads Phillip away, the text says, *"the eunuch did not see him again, but went on his way rejoicing."* We don't know for sure, but chances are, this man went on his way home to Ethiopia, newly changed by Christ and ready to tell others in Ethiopia about Him.

The power of this story is similar to the opportunity before Christian students today. Over 1.3 million college students are coming to America from other countries, and about two-thirds of those students coming from 10/40 window countries. Most of these international students are highly focused and motivated to study hard and finish their degree programs well, but many are also curious. They are curious about the world outside of their home country. I have met many who are curious to ask me very early in our relationship why I believe in Jesus. They tend to ask in a state of curiosity and not antagonism. The Ethiopian man was curious who the Scriptures were talking about and Phillip told him they were about Jesus and this man went home forever changed. It is also possible this man was the first Christian witness in the country of Ethiopia. The motivation for domestic students is they can be a blessing to the Kingdom by filling a similar role as Phillip on their college campuses. They could be someone God would use to explain Jesus to an international student so that when they go back to their home country, they will go on their way rejoicing and take the blessing of Jesus with them.

God has been blessing the church with creative access to countries within the 10/40 window

Inspiration for Action

Many 10/40 window countries are difficult territory for Christian missionaries. Access to enter these countries and rules by which a person must follow in order to stay in them has moved the Church to find more creative ways to bring the blessing of the Gospel to all ethnic groups. At the same time, in America, God has been blessing the Church with creative access to these countries. And today, that creative access is only increasing at a rapid pace on college campuses.

According to statistics from Open Doors USA, China is the largest sending country of international students. From the 2011-2012 school year to the 2012-2013 school year, the

Chinese college student population in America grew by 41,568.[90] In China, the government holds strict control over five officially recognized religions which includes Christianity; however, the government also holds high restraint against the expression of religious beliefs. Therefore, the dominant belief system in China is no belief system. As of 2010, about 44% of China was classified as Atheist. In the same year, 28.5% of Chinese people believed in some form of Chinese folk religion and another 12.5% believed in Buddhism. These three belief systems account for 85% of the country of China.[91] Due to the high government restraint on religious expression, the majority of Chinese people have never even heard of Jesus, let alone, been connected with other Christians. But God is creating access to China, a country that wants to limit religious beliefs and expression, by bringing college students from China to a place where religious expression is protected in America.

In the 2005-2006 school year, students from Saudi Arabia started coming to American universities in increasing numbers due to the Saudi Scholarship Program that was launched that year. In 2005-2006 the number of Saudi students studying in America was 3,448, and by the 2012-2013 school year, there were 44,556 students.[92] This is an increase of almost thirteen times since 2005. This Saudi Scholarship program is expected to last until the year 2020, and so this growth in Saudi students is expected to continue.

---

[90] Open Doors USA Data, *Fast Facts Open Doors 2013,* http://www.iie.org/Research-and-Publications/Open-Doors (accessed January 31, 2014).

[91] Jason Mandryk, editor, *Operation World: The Definitive Prayer Guide to Every Nation, 7th ed.* (Downers Grove: InterVarsity Press, 2012) 215.

[92] Open Doors USA Data, *Open Doors Fast Fact Sheet: Saudi Arabia,* http://www.iie.org/Research-and-Publications/Open-Doors/Data/Fact-Sheets-by-Country/2013 (accessed January 31, 2014).

Saudi Arabia is an Islamic state. *"People of faiths other than Islam can live in Saudi Arabia, but they may neither practice their religion openly nor gather privately."*[93] In 2010, this country was estimated to be 92% Muslim and only 5% Christian. To live in Saudi Arabia as a Christian is very difficult. *"Saudi Arabia's record on religious freedom and human rights is notorious and probably the world's worst. Abuses occur through a corrupt judicial system and through aggressive and ubiquitous religious police who operate with minimal accountability."*[94] As a result, Christians are persecuted or removed from the country. Yet, in a country where the free expression of faith in Jesus is restricted, God is bringing college students out of Saudi Arabia at a record pace. He is bringing them to America where they not only learn about their science of discipline but can also learn about Jesus if Christians will build bridges with them before they return home.

Prayer should be the beginning, the end and all through the middle of a ministry that attempts to lead domestic students to seize the opportunity at their university in reaching unreached international students.[95]

Local Church Ministry to International Students

Many campus ministries exist because there are local churches behind the scenes financially supporting the ministry, praying for it, and offering their resources when available and helpful. The Christian campus ministry at WIU

---

[93] Jason Mandryk, editor, *Operation World: The Definitive Prayer Guide to Every Nation, 7th ed.* (Downers Grove: InterVarsity Press, 2012) 728.
[94] Ibid, 729.
[95] Don Smith from Pittsburg State University strongly agreed with this discipline of prayer for international students as being the most important part of international student ministry during my interview with him.

has a partnership of 35 churches that help provide this type of support. However, ministries like the one mentioned at Missouri Southern State University in Joplin, MO is simply sponsored by one congregation, College Heights Christian Church. Whatever the relationship a campus ministry has with local churches, the local church is also a valuable resource a campus ministry leader can encourage to become active in reaching the different ethnic groups studying at a university.

Biblical Teaching on Evangelism for Local Church Members

The challenge for a campus ministry leader is offering the motivation for members of a local church to engage in actively ministering to international students. Many of the same cultural values of ethnocentrisms, nationalism and traditionalism are barriers to local church members engaging international people, just as they are barriers for domestic college students. At the same time, many university towns suffer from the social divide that exists between town and gown, keeping both sides from engaging the other in positive relationships.[96] Tapping into a motivation to actively minister to college students, regardless of their place of origin, is a difficult task for a ministry leader. But just as it is with domestic and international students, motivation for global evangelism in the local church begins with scripture.

A Gateway to the Nations: Acts 20 – Paul in Troas

In Acts 20:7-12, Paul is spending his last night with the church in Troas. They are meeting in a room on the third floor of a building there. In verse 7, the phrase, *"to break*

[96] Dictionary.com, http://dictionary.reference.com/browse/town+and+gown.

bread,"[97] is a common phrase to describe a formal gathering of people, sharing a meal.[98] During this gathering, Paul shared wisdom with them all night long. At some point, while Paul was still talking, a boy named Eutychus, gradually falls asleep while sitting in the window and tumbled out to his death.[99] Paul rushed to ground level and when he arrived, he took the child's body in his arms and commanded everyone to not be afraid and said, *"his life is in him."*[100] The assembly gathered again in the upper room, ate and conversed until daylight when Paul had to go. After he left, the people took Eutychus home alive.

The interesting thing about the city of Troas is its importance to world travel and trade in the first century. Troas was a major port city located on the northwest coastline of Asia Minor in the region of Mysia. It was a major gateway of goods and people passing from Asia to Europe. With this city being so important for trade and travel, would it not also make sense that this city could be the gateway for the gospel into the rest of the world as well? As the gospel message journeyed from Jerusalem through the Roman Empire, I'm convinced that this resurrection of Eutychus was a catalyst for the church at Troas being extremely influential in world evangelism. This local church not only knew the

World leaders, business people, medical professionals, engineers and more are passing though American college campuses in greater numbers

[97] Acts 20:7 (New American Standard Bible, 1995 Update).
[98] J. Swanson, *Dictionary of Biblical Languages with Semantic Domains : Greek (New Testament)* (electronic ed.) (Oak Harbor: Logos Research Systems, Inc., 1997), GGK3089.
[99] W. W. Wiersbe, The Bible Exposition Commentary: An Exposition of the New Testament Comprising the entire 'BE' series. (Wheaton: Victor Books, 1989.).
[100] Acts 20:10.

message of Christ's resurrection from the grave, but they also had personally witnessed the power of Christ, seeing resurrection with their own eyes. I think that God granted the resurrection of Eutychus from death in the presence of the church at Troas, to ignite their passion for sharing the Gospel. Because of the city's position in world trade and travel, this local church had the potential to influence the majority of the known world.

With growing and more diverse populations attending college in America, the modern-day Troas is on American campuses. World leaders, business people, medical professionals, engineers, and more are passing through American campuses in greater numbers every year according to the Institute of International Education. The opportunity to reach all the ethnic groups that Jesus desires the Gospel to reach is available. The challenge for the local church members near a university campus is to recognize this opportunity and become passionate about participating in these gateways to the world.

The local church is important to a campus ministry for the many resources they can provide, but campus ministry toward international students is an opportunity local church members need to be actively engaged in. It is an opportunity similar to Phillip who was called by God to minister to the Ethiopian without leaving the country. The same type of global mission opportunity exists for all Christians in America as people from all the nations keep coming here for education, and then going back to their home countries where they can testify to what they saw and heard.

Inspiration for Action

Research institutions like Purdue University have gathered that around 80% of international students never get the opportunity to see the inside of an American home.[101] This sounds ridiculous from the context of WIU where there are between 350 and 400 international students. However, at institutions like Purdue University and the University of Illinois, who have thousands of international students, the chances of the university placing all their international students in an American home is a much larger task.

In the summer of 2013, my family and I were convicted by this statistic and hosted a group of female students from South Korea for a weekend homestay program. We had met with these students for a potluck dinner a couple of weeks before the homestay, but other than this two-hour dinner, we had very little knowledge or comfort with them. However, my wife and I were surprised by the ease of the interaction. The first evening we cooked homemade pizza, American and Korean style. Then on Saturday, we took them to the zoo, and they played with our children while checking out all the zoo exhibits.

I talked with this student for over an hour about how we came to be followers of Jesus

On Saturday evening, one of the students asked me for some paper and a pen. She disappeared to the guest room and returned to the living room a short time later and asked my wife and I if she could ask us some questions. We sat down to talk, while our children played board games with the other two students. She told us that she was glad to have been placed in our home for the weekend because we were Christians and knew a lot about the local church. She was not a Christian, but she was doing a report in her college class

[101] Purdue University, International Students and Scholars: International Friends Club, http://www.iss.purdue.edu/Programs/IFP/ (accessed March 16, 2014).

about the church in America. From this opening statement, my wife and I talked with this student for over an hour, not just about the local church, but also how we came to be followers of Jesus and how we hoped that she would find the same to be true herself.

Language Concerns

One of the more common fears local church members have in relation to communicating with international students is a simple fear of communication. Some international students are still learning basic English, where others have strong accents that make English hard to understand for an American. One of the great victories as a result of technological advances is easy to use translating apps available on most smartphones. These apps allow a user to translate English into a number of other languages, as well as translate other languages into English. Two popular apps are *iTranslate* by Sonico GmbH and *Google Translate* by Google, Inc. Both apps are free downloads from the App Store and *Google Translate* is free from Google Play. In the past year, I have noticed that these smartphone apps are carried by most international students, so local church members can ease their fear over communication struggles because if something is not clear, the student's smartphone will probably have a solution.

Application for Action

There are several ministries who are leading their local church members to engage international students. Some are more interactive than others, but if language barriers are not something that have to be of concern, then what are some examples of ways local church members can have an active role in international student ministry?

The Value of the American Home

In the previously mentioned research by Purdue University, about 80% of international students never get to see an American home. In my interactions with international students, this experience is something most desire to have while in America. Many universities have programs designed to make this happen. *"Purdue University's International Friendship Program provides the opportunity for local residents to open their homes and hearts to international students and experience a whole new world."*[102] WIU has a similar program called *International Neighbors. "This program allows the students to teach community members more about their country and culture, but it also allows the new students to learn about U.S. culture while giving them meaningful contact with community members."*[103] From a Christian perspective, that meaningful contact is only meaningful if it has lasting value. Programs like this are available at many universities where community members volunteer to spend time with an international student at least one time each month during a semester. These relationships are meant to help an international student in their first semester, but many times, last beyond the academic career of the student. These monthly activities can include dinner at home, taking in a baseball game, shopping, or anything that encourages interaction and communication. This could even include events at a local member's home church.

---

[102] Purdue University, International Students and Scholars: International Friends Club, http://www.iss.purdue.edu/Programs/IFP/ (accessed March 16, 2014).

[103] Western Illinois University, International Studies: Community Activities, http://www.wiu.edu/international_studies/student_activities/Community-Activities.php (accessed March 21, 2014).

Holiday Adoption

In addition to this university program, something Crossroads International Student Ministry advocates for is American families taking in international students to let them experience an American Christmas or Thanksgiving. For international students who do not get invited to go home with a domestic student during academic breaks, the majority are left on campus. Any major holiday celebrated by American's is a time that most international students enjoy getting to experience American culture.

> *This was the most special Thanksgiving celebration they had ever had*

A family in Roseville, IL decided to make adopting international students a priority for Thanksgiving. Their daughter attended the University of Illinois where she had met two Chinese students, whom she brought home for the break. This family also contacted the ministry at WIU and connected with a Nigerian student and Bolivian student, whom they also invited for Thanksgiving dinner. Before dinner was served, the mother of the family explained what Thanksgiving is all about. She also explained to everyone that Jesus is the real reason she has anything to be thankful for. In the midst of these international students getting to experience a significant holiday in American culture, they also had seeds of the Gospel planted in their minds. This family expressed to me that this was the most special Thanksgiving celebration they had ever had.

Moving Crew

International students are mostly dependent upon what is available by walking, biking or taking public transportation. For the most part, all college students can survive without their own vehicle for transportation, but when it comes to move-in and move-out time, this can be a stressful experience for international students when they do not have personal transportation or family resources easily available. This need has sparked some campus ministries to coordinate moving crew help to aid the transitions for international students.

A meaningful relationship building time is helping international students move when they have a need. Local church members who have trucks, trailers and large vans can serve as hero's to many international students and provide a favor they will not soon forget. Helping international students move has been one of the key places I have met international students for the first time. Second interactions and invitations become easier after making an initial contact while helping them or their friend move.

American Culture Experiences

Don Smith is an International Student Minister at Pittsburg State University in Kansas. He tries to network with local Christians to provide American cultural experiences for international students. Some of these events include fishing trips, farm tours and bonfires. The events are not billed as ministry or Christian events, however, Don makes sure that the people who are leading these events are Christian people to help start a relationship that might move to a more meaningful relationship.

Another example is hosting an educational Super Bowl party. For most international students, American football is a foreign sport, but a huge part of American culture. No football event is bigger than the Super Bowl and international students tend to be curious about this major event. Some ministries, including Christ on Campus at the

University of Arkansas, have taken to organizing a Super Bowl party that begins with an education on the game of American football before the game begins. This way the international students can understand what is going on during the game as they also enjoy the atmosphere of a Super Bowl party. This is an idea that can happen in a home as well.

Transportation is a basic need for international students

Furniture and Bicycle Ministries

International students usually arrive at their new university with only the items they could bring on a plane. For those who live off-campus, they typically need access to furniture for their apartment or house. Since they are only staying for a short while, having easy and inexpensive access to furniture is a special resource for international students. The Christian Campus House at the University of Missouri partners with their local churches to create a furniture lending program for international students. Local church members who have used furniture in good condition can donate it to the ministry who will then have it available to international students when they have a need. The news of this generosity has spread among the international student population, and the relationships continue to grow as more international students come to the Christian Campus House for furniture help.

Basic transportation is also a need for international students. For a larger campus like the University of Missouri, bicycles are in high demand by international students. This program is like the furniture ministry where local church members who have used and good working bicycles can donate them to the Christian Campus House, and the ministry will lend them out to international students who have need. Word about this generous service spreads as well.

Taking the Next Step

Jesus trained his disciples by taking them everywhere he went, showing them, encouraging them and releasing them to make disciples. Barnabas followed that same model as he mentored Saul who became a highly effective cross-cultural minister. A similar model can be followed by a Christian leader who is trying to lead local church members to make disciples of international students. When an event is planned to minister to international students, a Christian leader would be wise to invite some local church members to come participate and experience the blessing. The hardest part of engaging local church members in international student ministry is simply getting them to start. Most who start taking an active role in international student ministry receive so much blessing in return that it fuels them to continue making efforts and striving for chances to plant seeds of the gospel in the lives of international students.

From Bridges to the Cross

"How, then, can they call on the one they have not believed in? And how can they believe in the one of whom they have not heard? And how can they hear without someone preaching to them? And how can they preach unless they are sent? As it is written, "How beautiful are the feet of those who bring good news!" But not all the Israelites accepted the good news. For Isaiah says, "Lord, who has believed our message?" Consequently, faith comes from hearing the message, and the message is heard through the word of Christ." (Romans 10:14-17, NIV84)

Building relationships with international students is the first difficult step in international student ministry, but the point of Christian ministry is not just building relationships from person to person, but helping people build a relationship with Jesus Christ. Those who bring the good news to the foreign field are beautiful people, but just as Paul exclaims, anyone who brings the good news to unreached people is beautiful. Since Jesus desires for the Gospel to reach all the ethnic groups, participation in this beautiful work is available very close to everyone's front door in America.

She came from China and had never heard of Jesus

Leading people to engage the different ethnic groups on college campuses is going to be different from one campus to another. A single approach from one campus might not be as successful at the next. Part of a Christian leader's job who desires to lead others to engage in this special ministry is to understand the different ethnic groups that are living in their specific context, and become better prepared to minister and lead others to minister to those specific groups. One example I've noticed is the difference between Chinese students and Saudi students. Most Chinese students are comfortable and aware of different religious beliefs whether they have one or they are an Atheist. Saudi students, however, are very comfortable with their Muslim belief system, and not as much with other belief systems. A Christian who wishes to share the Gospel with students from different parts of the world would be wise to consider different approaches to minimize confusion or offenses.

The Apostle Paul said of himself: *"To the Jews I became like a Jew, to win the Jews. To those under the law, I became like one under the law (though I myself am not under the law), so as to win those under the law. To those not having the law I became like one not having the law (though I am not free from God's law but am under Christ's law), so as to win those not having the law. To the weak I became weak, to win the weak. I have become all things to all men so that by all possible means I might save some. I do all this for the sake of the gospel, that I may share in its blessings."* (1 Corinthians 9:20-23)

Yang came to WIU in the fall of 2011 from China where she had never met a Christian, nor had she heard of Jesus. When she arrived on campus, she started her Master of Arts degree with a week of New International Student Orientation where she met two American students who desired to share Jesus with her. Both students continued to meet with Yang in formal and informal settings. One of them became Yang's conversational English partner who met with her every week to practice speaking and reading English. Since Yang seemed open to it, the student gave Yang a Bible and they read it together. As their relationship grew, Yang was invited to attend Sunday morning worship with this student. Slowly, Yang met other Christian students and she began to embrace this community of Christian people. During Yang's second school year, she moved into an apartment with the student who had helped her learn English and two other female Christian students. At the end of the second school year, this same student who met Yang in the beginning, immersed her into Christ.

Yang's story continues beyond WIU. She now lives in Hayward, CA, which is a town located outside of Oakland. Hayward is a town of 144,000 people in a county of over 1.5 million, according to the 2010 census data.[104] In that same

[104] The City of Hayward, *A Summary of the 2010 Census: Selected Population, Demographic and Housing Characteristics,*

year, 17.7% of Hayward was populated by Chinese people. Yang said one of the biggest lessons she learned from the campus ministry at WIU was the importance of sharing her new faith in Jesus with others who needed to know. Yang has a new mission field full of people who are just like who she used to be, yet able to speak to that 17.7% of Hayward as an insider, much like I expect that Ethiopian Eunuch did to his own countrymen after he met Phillip on the road down to Gaza.

Barry Reed (B.S. in Accountancy - Western Illinois University; M.A. in Leadership Studies - Lincoln Christian University) served for 12 years as Director of Campus Ministries with Campus Students for Christ at Western Illinois University in Macomb, IL. During those twelve years, the ministry at WIU evolved from a 1% international student population, to being 50% international students among the student membership. In 2019, Barry joined the staff of Fellowship Associates for Medical Evangelism (FAME) to engage in medical evangelism as the Director of Mission Resources.

---

http://www.hayward-ca.gov/CITY-GOVERNMENT/documents/pdf/Census_Summary_2010.pdf (accessed March 24, 2014) 5.

Chapter 12

CARING FOR THE MUSLIM STUDENT

By Rose Ann

"I always thought you had a bomb in your pocket. That's why I was afraid to be your friend." James finally shared his true feelings with Ahmed. It took over a year living next door on a university campus for their friendship to begin.

James was not the only one with misconceptions. "I thought Christians partied, slept around and hated Muslims," Ahmed revealed his own thoughts. "But after watching you I knew this wasn't true."

Stories like this are not uncommon as Muslim students are now on American campuses in record numbers. What a timely opportunity for Christians to reach out in friendship and hospitality to welcome these students, many from countries which attempt to severely restrict them from hearing the good news of Jesus. Yet, these very students are often viewed suspiciously and shunned. The opportunity for deep and lasting relationship is rich but often never taken; the doors into Muslim students' lives never opened. Taking the time and investing in friendships with Muslim students, can bring about amazing results. Al Fadi, Sahar, and Nasser are living examples of the eternal difference that was made when Christians moved into their lives.

Al Fadi

Growing up as a strict Wahabi Muslim in Saudi Arabia, it wasn't a surprise that Al Fadi asked his parents for permission to fight jihad in Afghanistan. When his parents said, "No," Al Fadi decided instead to come to America, study engineering, and take part in another type of 'holy war' by infiltrating the American church to spread Islam while on his student visa.

Though Al Fadi spoke excellent English, soon after arriving in America he decided to sharpen his language skills even more and become familiar with idioms. He signed up for the Friendship Family program advertised at his university. A Christian family befriended Al Fadi and became the first followers of Jesus he would meet. They helped him with idioms and also helped Al Fadi see that Christians are very different than what he had been taught in his Islamic studies. They were very kind and caring people. They lived devout lives. They honored God.

He began to question his religion

In a few months, Al Fadi began to question his religion. Questioning Islam is a sin, yet the Christians he met were so loving and kind. What was going on? After ten years of continued struggle, Al Fadi made the decision to forsake all and follow Jesus.

Al Fadi lost touch with the family that influenced him and it was years before he was able to reconnect with them and thank them for all they had done. When they finally met after 10 years, this dedicated family shared that they were still praying for Al Fadi, but had stopped reaching out to international students because they felt they had been ineffective.

Sahar

Sahar was raised in a strict Saudi family structure. The death of her father prompted a deep longing for a different life.

"Finally, that day came... I took the opportunity to come to the United States as a part of the Saudi government scholarship program, to leave behind the obvious challenges and narrow perspectives that women face in Saudi, and to obtain a higher quality of education. Leaving Saudi was like a dream to me. I felt like a prisoner leaving a jail and that life had just begun. I was desperate for freedom from depression and the hopeless life I had!"

Sahar loved studying in America and experiencing freedoms unknown in her home country. This freedom also allowed Sahar to question her religion of Islam. One day a Christian named Cynthia was passing out calendars on campus and befriended Sahar. Though Cynthia lived an hour away, they met regularly for coffee and lunch. Sahar was drawn to the peace and joy she saw in Cynthia. Cynthia often shared the reason for this peace. Sahar would draw near, read the Bible, then become afraid and not answer texts or phone calls from Cynthia for months. Cynthia faithfully continued to pray for and reach out in love to Sahar, while also giving her the space she was needing to process the next steps in her faith journey. Cynthia even arranged for Sahar to meet with Nabeel Qureshi *(author of Seeking Allah Finding Jesus)* and other Muslim background believers. This was a tremendous help to Sahar as she could ask questions directly to those that struggled with the same questions she was having. Six years after Sahar met

She was needing to process the next steps in her faith journey

Cynthia, Sahar made the decision to follow Jesus, and now she knows personally the peace and joy she saw in Cynthia. Sahar currently works with a campus ministry and freely shares her story with other Muslims.

Nasser

Nasser was raised in the Middle East, but due to the threat of war in his country, his family moved to America where Nasser attended junior high school. Things were rough trying to be a devout Muslim in an American town in the Midwest. Once someone even hid pork in Nasser's food to show him nothing bad would happen if he ate the banned meat. High school proved equally difficult. Nasser found that living as a Muslim among a Christian majority was lonely and arduous, yet he remained devout.

It took months, but he finally agreed to come to church

Throughout his school years, Nasser shared his Islamic beliefs with many Christians. He found Christians were unprepared for the challenge he posed to their beliefs. A few Christians were even persuaded to become Muslim. His future wife, Daisy, showed interest in Islam, but decided to remain Christian.

They agreed this was fine, married, but life did not go smoothly as planned.

Daisy thought they would raise their daughter to be a Christian, but now to her shock and dismay, Nasser revealed that he had no plans for their daughter other than Islam. Daisy was heartbroken. She loved her husband but was distraught with this turn in their relationship and the understanding she thought she had about how their children would be raised.

Daisy turned back wholeheartedly to Jesus and joined a Bible study with loving women that cared and prayed for her and diligently prayed for her husband.

It took months, but finally, Nasser agreed to come to church. Thinking it would be beneficial to see first-hand the weaknesses in Christian sermons, Nasser attended church, certain it would help him convert more Christians to Islam. Going to church with Daisy would also make her happier. It was a 'win-win' for them.

In time, Nasser began to struggle in his thinking. Songs and verses he heard in church would remain in his mind and resurface during the week. He also noticed he was very judgmental towards other Muslims. They were not as good as he, a Saudi Muslim. This bothered Nasser because he knew Muslims prided themselves on oneness, yet his heart was very divisive.

One Sunday while sitting in a church service, Nasser had a vision of Jesus. The struggle was over. He knew he was a sinner and that Jesus died for his sins. Nasser turned his life over to Jesus and has been sharing his story with those who will listen ever since. He urges us as American believers in Jesus to move towards those who are Muslim and to become involved in their lives, knowing first-hand the power of God's love, prayer and the Spirit of God to touch hearts and change minds of those who seem totally committed to their religion.

Look for friends, not ministry projects

As follower of Jesus, we are commanded to welcome the foreigner and stranger and show hospitality (Hebrews 13:2). This is not optional for us. Yet, how do we overcome our misconceptions and take the first step? How do we help others join us in this? Sometimes we don't do anything because we don't know what to do. Good things happen when, in faith and the power of the Spirit, we just start!

One Family's Story

Jim and Leah have seven children and were hesitant at first about inviting a stranger into their home. They eventually decided to sign up to share a meal or family event with an international student at least once a month. They tell their story.

"Last summer I saw the post in the bulletin about Friendship Families. I immediately thought it sounded like a fun idea. I thought it would be a great way to introduce my kids to the world right here in our own home. I never imagined how much God was about to grow my family's hearts...

We were assigned a student from the Middle East. I will be honest, when I first saw where he was from, my heart skipped a few beats. I had my share of fears in regard to those from the Middle East. Still, I was excited to meet our new student.

We have developed a very special relationship with our student. He has been to our home multiple times for dinner, to surprise us with fun gifts, to play games, and just to hang out. Over Christmas, he and a friend went with us to celebrate with our family and to learn some of our traditions. He seems to fit perfectly with our family, maybe because he is from a large family and we have seven children! We are a large, loud, and energetic family which often is mind blowing to some, but he thinks we are normal!

He has become a part of our family. Our kids refer to him as their brother, I call him "son," and he calls me "mom." He proudly introduces us to his friends as his family.

There are things for which I will be forever grateful for. Our student has shown us how important family is, what it means to be very hospitable, and what it means to give someone else your very best. He loves our children in such an amazing way."

Serving alongside families like this has been a wonderful experience for me. University students have also been an example of intentionally loving and caring for their Muslim friends.

Experience is a great teacher. Here are the best practices we would like to share that come from what we have learned from each other, from our mistakes, and from doing a few things right over the past several years of working with Muslim students.

Honor Those You are Seeking to Serve

Our intention is love - not conversion. Our duty is to love our neighbor, honor them, and then allow God to open doors to conversation about spiritual matters. They quickly detect when we have a goal to achieve rather than authentic friendship. If they sense you want to convert them or change them, they will immediately be on the defensive. If they sense this, they may put up further walls of defense towards you. Approach the relationship lovingly pursuing them and they are more willing to share their life with you and will want to hear about your life as well. Look for friends, not ministry projects.

Be Honest about Who You Are

They expect you to be different than them so don't try to be like them to fit in or to feel more comfortable around them. They want to see what you and your faith are all about.

Be a good listener and learn about who they are, but don't be afraid to share who you are and what you believe. We can be bold in our faith but our presentation needs to be thoughtful and considerate – not belittling of them. Don't shy away from conversations about your faith; they may be very curious to hear what Christians really believe. If Jesus is the most important person to you, He should naturally enter your conversations.

Be family to them.

Invite your Muslim friend to family events. They are usually from large families and love multiple generations getting together. They often think Americans don't value family, so they will be pleasantly surprised when invited to family gatherings.

Focus on Your Strengths

God has given each person a special mixture of gifts and interests. Share these with your Muslim friend. Whether it be music, art, outdoor adventures, or sports, your international friend usually wants to learn more about what Americans are like. Being friends with a Muslim is not rocket science. Just be yourself.

Humbly Meet with Them

Take the offer to sit in their home and eat their food while intently and patiently listening to their stories. Don't try to manipulate the conversation to show how you are right and they are wrong. Get to know them and build a relationship.

Be Available to Help with the Ordinary Needs of Life

Needs include finding apartments, furniture, trips to the airport, medical visits, finding halal foods, and even connecting them with a source for buying goat meat can be a real help. Females may even enjoy trying to drive.

Just Show Up!

You don't have to be extraordinarily gifted with relational skills. Be a consistent and faithful friend. This deepens trust and binds hearts together. Most long-lasting relationships with Muslim students come from being a consistent and trustworthy friend.

When in doubt, ask questions

Sometimes I've felt stuck in a conversation, so I try to ask questions. How do you see forgiveness? As a Muslim, do you ever know for sure if you will go to heaven? You seem like a peaceful Muslim, can you explain what the Quran says about jihad?

If You See a Muslim Student, Introduce Yourself!

Be ready to say, "Salaam Alecum," and ask how they are doing. See if they need help finding something or if they are a new student. They really just want to be considered and noticed. Don't single out Muslims. It's pretty fishy if in a group of international students you only talk to those that are Muslim. Jesus desires all people to come to him, not just Muslims. Don't get so hyper-focused that you forget to witness to everyone around you.

Meetings and Time

If They Invite you over for Dinner, to a Party, Baby Shower or Birthday Party -- GO!

They are not just "being polite" like we do in our culture. They are asking out of respect for you, but also because they want you to come. This is also the best way to meet other Muslim students and potentially older members of their community as well. They don't throw small parties or short ones, so be prepared to introduce yourself and be there a while. Take a nap before going if you need to – some parties may not start until after 11 pm.

Be Relaxed and Flexible about Time

As Americans, we value punctuality and have a very fast flowing agenda. We want to accomplish one event and move on to the next. However, this does not work well for building relationships with our Muslim friends. Time moves more slowly because relationships are the priority for them. They are nocturnal and evenings are often the best time for getting together Take a nap so you can plan to stay up late and enjoy their company.

Don't be Offended if they Don't Show Up or Respond to Invitations

They do not want to tell you 'no' and might rather say "yes" but not show up. Don't be offended by no shows, time changes or tardiness. Sometimes students get busy and forget. Sometimes something else has come up and they don't want to offend you by explaining the situation. Be flexible.

Culture Differences

Be Modest and Respect Cultural Boundaries between Male and Female

Be prepared to hug and shake hands woman to woman, or man to man, but never the opposite gender. When eating a meal together, some Muslims are more comfortable if men and women eat at separate tables. Muslim men may be uncomfortable answering questions about their wives or female family members in front of other males.

Be Mindful of Male and Female Boundaries

Men, don't approach a Muslim woman for a hug or to shake her hand. Women- don't make the mistake of shaking the hand of a female friend's husband! Things like this can be misunderstood and you'll know as you see the look of horror on your friend's face.

If the Topic of Politics Comes up, be Willing to Admit Weaknesses in our Own System

Politics is a hot topic with Muslims and eventually will surface. Ask questions and you will learn a whole new view of the world and its problems.

Be Conscious of Social Networks in Muslim Communities

Most Muslim groups will keep a tight watch on each other to make sure no one is out of line. There is a better opportunity to go deeper into spiritual matters in a smaller group setting.

Women - Beware of Taking Part in the Gossip that Happens among Women

They are just like other women in that they have disputes with one another, and they like to talk about it behind the scenes. Model healthy ways to deal with conflict and share how this approach comes from a relationship with Jesus.

Don't Underestimate their Fear of Dogs

The Quran says dogs are very dirty and can interfere with their prayers. Keep dogs outside or out of sight. I have seen women scream and run if a dog entered the room. To better understand, try to imagine what you would feel like if someone had a pet pig in their house.

Education

Study Up on Their Culture

Be aware of their specific country of origin, family background, their personal interests, etc. as you will need to connect on multiple layers. A Saudi Muslim is vastly different from a Yemeni Muslim. Shia are different from Sunnis. There are also different tribes within each major group and some do not like to mix. Be aware that there is a set of canned answers to religious-oriented questions. Engaging their eastern thinking with our western analytic approach makes for challenging conversations. Work at getting them to think about questions more deeply than what they've memorized in their Islamic rote learning.

Ask Questions to Better Understand Rather than Argue about Differences

They often want to talk about politics and religion but let them lead and talk, then ask questions and try not to give answers. Arguments drive a wedge between you and your friend. Avoid saying, “I doubt that" or "I'm sure that's not the way it happened.” Be okay with saying, "Oh that's interesting," or "That was a sad situation." Words like these diffuse rather than incite. The truth is people of our religion have done some quite surprisingly, negative things in the past and even today. In religious discussions, it is best to not attack Mohammed or the Quran.

Educate Yourself about Islam

This is part of our need to be "prepared in season and out." You don't need to be an expert on all the issues, but you need to have a working knowledge about their religion. This is one way to understand their worldview. What is halal meat? What is Ramadan? Eid? These are terms you will hear as your friendship develops. Read books, ask questions, and go to seminars like Crescent Project's Bridges or Oasis Seminar

Hospitality

Share Meals and Cook Together Often

Take advantage of every opportunity to share a meal. Wherever Jesus went, there seemed to be food and/or drink. Cooking together is also a great connector. It's helpful to know if you are invited to eat with them, the food preparations may not begin until after you arrive and have a cup of tea. Be aware that most Muslims do not eat pork or pork products like gelatin and marshmallows.

The Importance of Hospitality

Islam came from the Middle East where hospitality meant life or death. If a traveler was not welcomed in, they might not survive the desert elements. It is a beautiful part of their culture. When we practice hospitality, we are speaking a language with which they are very familiar.

Look for Ways to Celebrate

Birthday parties, baby showers, picnics, holidays and cultural events are a great way to create fun memories. Ask about their holidays also, and see if there are ways you can share in events like meals to break fast during Ramadan.

Faith

Pray

Ask God to show you what you can do to love and honor your Muslim friend. Pray over the conversations and interactions that you will have with your friend. Also, share with them answered prayer in your own life. Pray with them after you have developed trust in the relationship and they consent to you praying with them. One family said, "You are less likely to offend a Muslim through prayer than an American."

Be Patient in Spiritual Matters

A Muslim friend of ours had a dream and a vision about Jesus, yet is still unsure about following Him. It takes, on average, 2-7 years for a Muslim to make a decision to follow Jesus. Islam is woven into every fiber of their lives. Don't expect things to happen overnight or you will be disappointed.

Remember that Islam is Not the Enemy- Satan is

Islam is a religion closely tied to Christianity (Jesus and the Truth) and Satan has crafted within it lies connected to truth. This makes it all the more dangerous because there is truth and wisdom in Islam, but the lies choke the truth. Ultimately, this is not "us" versus "them," rather we are both fighting the common enemy of the devil. Do your best to remember that important truth.

Be Ready to Share your Faith

Share the ways God is working around you and how Jesus influences your daily decisions. Don't fear rejection. Beware of shallow conversations that become comfortable but go nowhere. If we truly believe that we have the Truth that will set people free from bondage and give eternal life, we won't keep silent! We must speak out in love.

Ask if They have Questions about Jesus or Christianity

This is a great approach that will give you a window into where they are in their view of Jesus by the questions they ask. Don't be shy in dialoguing about the questions they raise, and if you don't know the answer, tell them so. But seek out the answer to their question as best you can.

Share Stories from the Old Testament with Them

This will help them better understand why Jesus needed to come and what his role is in salvation. His Word does not return void, so keep this in mind as opportunities arise to share scripture.

Be Sensitive about Inviting Them to Church

For some Muslims, the American church experience can be very offensive. Women and men mixed, women on stage, people wearing shoes into a place of worship… these are only a few of the cultural things they may question. If they are to see Jesus, they need to see Him in a way they understand. Because of their cultural background or country of origin, some students may have more difficulty accepting an invitation to a Christian event. Still, others may be more willing to join you since their devotion to Islam is less rigid.

Talk about Jesus Often

They believe Jesus was a prophet and healer so talk about Him. Tell stories about the life of Jesus. Don't try to defend the history of the church or Christianity, but do talk about the goodness and forgiveness of Jesus.

Reaching Out as Jesus Did

Caring for the Muslim international student is not easy. If it was easy, there would be a lot of people engaging with them. With a compassionate heart and an open home, you can make a difference in the lives of those who are earnestly seeking God but come from a much different starting point.

Jesus continually reached out to the outcast and marginalized. You can too.

Rose Ann wrote this chapter to encourage readers to put aside their fears and reach the nations in our backyard. She has lived in a Muslim country, shared her home with international students and refugees and helped countless Americans learn how to better share Christ's love with the strangers among us.

Chapter 13

STARTING AN ENGLISH CONVERSATION CLUB ON CAMPUS

By Greg Swinney

Yun just wanted to make an American friend. The wife of a visiting scholar, she felt more alone in the United States than at any time in her life. Her English skills were fair as a result of her years of studying English in China, but her conversational skills were lacking. There were few opportunities for her to practice listening and pronouncing her new English vocabulary words while her husband was away working at the nearby university. She couldn't think of any options. Walking through the Library at the local University, she spotted a poster advertising "English Corner." A student organization on campus there in Gainesville, Florida, was hosting an English conversation group for a few afternoons a week. Later that week, she grabbed the hand of her young 10-year-old daughter and nervously headed for the meeting.

> *"How can I make and American friend?" she asked*

I met Yun at that meeting and, like so many Chinese visitors, she was engaging and inquisitive. *"How can I make an American friend?"* she asked. I was surprised when she began to apologize for Americans. *"I know that Americans are busy, and have many responsibilities. They have their own lives to live. But I just want to make a friend. How can I do that?"* We talked for some time and didn't leave the campus ministry building before smiling for a cell phone photo and promising to keep in touch.

Why a Conversational English Club is Needed

Whatever you call it - an English Club, Conversation Table, English Corner or Talk it over Group is a place for language learners to gather to improve their English in a casual setting. Many have studied in a classroom setting and learned the basics. But there is no substitute for sitting around a table and just listening and responding. Classrooms are the perfect setting for learning grammar, vocabulary, and verb conjugation. But a conversation group offers a fresh dimension in the setting of casual conversation in a real-life situation.

Starting an English Club is a great way to open the door to new and lasting friendships. My involvement with conversation clubs has spanned for nearly two decades. Seeing the confidence of a young international student grow as his English pronunciation is practiced deepened our friendship and bonded us in a non-threatening atmosphere.

Why are English conversation clubs so popular?

Because speaking is possibly the most difficult language skill to master, it requires a lot of practice time. Some think it is much more difficult than reading or writing or even listening. To practice speaking and correctly pronouncing words a student needs something – a partner. Learners can talk to themselves or they can memorize dialogues and repeat them out loud, but it doesn't include the spontaneity of a conversation, the variety of possible accents, or the smile of a nearby friend.

English conversation clubs meet a social need. Typical members of conversation clubs are university students looking to practice English for travel. Older people are often looking to meet like-minded souls who've lived abroad or who've traveled extensively as they have. Getting these people together helps make natural connections.

How can I Start an English Club?

Select a Day

Finding the most convenient day to meet seems like a simple place to start. You might be surprised how complicated that really is. College schedules seem to gravitate towards a Monday-Wednesday-Friday or Tuesday-Thursday lifestyle. I like Thursday afternoons, but others find Saturday morning or Sunday evening a more convenient day. Once you select a good day of the week, be flexible. At your first meeting ask participants if a different day of the week would work better for them.

Be flexible to make adjustments along the way

The Best Time to Meet

Choose a meeting time that is convenient for the group can be challenging as well. Students have chaotic schedules and finding a common time for people to meet takes creative thought. Usually, late afternoons, evenings, or weekend days are chosen so the meetings don't conflict with work or school. The time you choose will also depend on when the room/space is available. During your introductory meeting find out when the most convenient time is for the majority of the members. If you make your meetings too early or too late, you may find that people come to the first few meetings and then drop out so be flexible to make adjustments along the way.

How Often Should the Group Meet

Foreign students and immigrants have busy schedules, as do most English-speaking volunteers. Some clubs fail because they expect too much of the members. Meeting once a week for about an hour (no longer than 90 minutes) is a good start. Balancing work, family, classes, and homework can be overwhelming for most students. Starting with a realistic time frame for meetings helps students fit one more meeting into their already hectic schedule. Some English Clubs also meet for an additional excursion once a month. As you make friends you may notice that people connect at a deeper level and may begin to get together in pairs or smaller groups outside of the club meetings.

What Location Would Work Best for Our English Club?

Finding a room that accommodates ten to twenty people should be adequate. Many leaders like to have a whiteboard for jotting down topics or a new vocabulary word. Scratch paper and pens scattered around the tables give students the tools to write things down, draw pictures, and even exchange contact information.

Fun places are always noisy

It's going to be noisy and animated as the conversations get going and laughter builds. I've been in a setting where we had over 220 students from forty different nations meeting for conversation and you can imagine the noise level of that group. Fun places are always noisy. Try to do a good job of arranging chairs or tables in smaller groups of 4-6 and there won't be a need for anyone to shout across a big table to be heard. There are many possible meeting locations and each has advantages and disadvantages.

A Classroom at the University

The easiest place to hold an English Club is in a spare classroom at a nearby university. After classroom hours, most schools remain open for an hour or two so that teachers can prepare for their classes. This is also a convenient location because some or all of the members will already be at the college and will have no excuses for missing a club meeting. You may also be given access to materials and television equipment. Still, students may feel like this setting is just a longer class period and they may already be tired from the class they just finished.

A casual setting can work very well

The Student Union or Library at the University

The Student Union at the university is a natural gathering place. Many universities have small meeting rooms in the Student Union or even food court areas could be a nice setting for casual discussion. Don't be surprised if a student brings a Subway sandwich to snack on during the meeting. This is a casual setting and can work very well if the area isn't located in a high traffic area where distractions come easily.

A Coffeeshop or Cafe near the College

Coffee shops or a restaurant work great. However, this type of setting will likely involve some cost. The manager may allow you to reserve a small room in the back if you choose a time of day when there are few customers. You will likely be expected to purchase beverages and tip a server, and you should expect this since you are using their space.

Operating your club out of a cafe may make it difficult to incorporate movies, music, and other listening practice.

Someone's Home

Taking your group out of the classroom and away from the university to make it feel less academic and more social is also a winning idea. If you decide to operate your club from a personal home, try to find more than one person who is willing to host the meetings. You will need to choose homes that are in a central location. Within the home, choose a room with a lot of space and few distractions. Serving coffee or tea or light snacks really add to the dynamic and can even get people talking much easier.

Providing transportation to and from an off-campus location takes some organization. Most international students don't own cars but depend on public transportation or bicycles. If the houses where you host the meeting are near a bus line or close to the campus you can enjoy hosting your meetings in homes.

Outdoors

One of the best places to hold an English Club is outside. This may only be possible during certain warm months depending on where you are located in the country. Choose a location where shelter can be found in case of rain or bright sunshine. Though the beach might sound like a great place to practice your English, remember that you might want to use pens and paper to make notes or drawings and that can be difficult in the breeze. A park with picnic tables and shady trees suit your group much better.

Consider the Atmosphere

Wherever you hold your club, remember that it is a social gathering, not a class. A pot of coffee or a bowl of popcorn can also make the meeting feel more like a club than a class. Why not encourage members to take off their shoes when they walk in the door or sit on the floor instead of chairs. Remember, the purpose of the club is to use English in a life-like situation. Do what feels natural and comfortable.

In the last three years, Cordell and Harrington have assisted students in overcoming language difficulties. They have answered questions about the meanings and usages of different words and phrases, cultural differences and taboos, and, ultimately, assisted students to develop socially and academically.

"We have five or six words in English for every one meaning," said Harrington at one of the latest meetings. "International students have often complained to me, 'Why does the English language have so many words that mean the same thing?'"

> *Include the time and place and a contact email on your publicity*

During one of their meetings, students raised questions about several words that mean the same thing: moldy, stale, and spoiled. "Not all of these adjectives mean the same thing," Harrington said. Words can overlap but not completely.

Inevitably, conversations will move to deeper topics. Faith, politics, relationships, and culture will be on the minds (and the tongues) of those in the group. Embrace it. Still, setting ground rules for civility and the free-flow of ideas will be a good policy to enact.

Make Publicity a Priority

Letting people know where, when, and how long is essential for the success of your English Conversation Club. Some campus ministries begin by simply putting a poster up in the student union or library on their campus. Local coffee shops usually have bulletin boards that are plastered with opportunities. Including the time and place and a contact email or cell phone number are important things to include on the poster. We usually include a "tear-off" tab at the bottom to make it easier for students to keep a reminder of where and when. Still, with cell phone cameras today, most internationals who are interested in your club will snap a picture on their phone. With any luck, they will forward it to a few friends and all walk together to your location. When they arrive be sure to have them share their contact information so you can invite them to future club meetings or any special events (i.e. Thanksgiving meal, local Zoo) you might host.

Here is a sample posting on by one group through a social media outlet:

The International Student Fellowship Club sponsors the English Conversation Table. With the intent to provide friendship and a better understanding of culture and positive educational experiences, the ISFC and Conversation Table provides a positive outlet for international students. We meet at the Student Union in the Cedar room every Thursday from 4:00 to 5:00 pm.

Share the Blessing by Enlisting Volunteers

Don't try to do everything yourself. You will want to find other native English speakers who will volunteer to come to your meetings. Retired folks or a high school student may be willing to help you. Some choose to place an ad in the college newspaper or at the library or supermarket.

"**WANTED**: Volunteer to help with English Club. Must be fluent in English. No teaching experience or preparation necessary. Call Bob at 333-3333 for more information."

At Your First Meeting

After you have enough people sign up (6-10 people is a good number) you will need to hold an introductory meeting. At the first meeting, members can learn each other's names and you can talk about what kind of club people are interested in. One way to organize the club is by putting one member in charge of being the host each week. They become a one-person welcome committee and set up the tables and chairs. Later, they can help clean up and throw away any left over papers or trash and ensure that no one leaves a cell phone or backpack. As you rotate the host for each week, they can even bring a snack from their home country or offer the topic for discussion that week. Ownership within the group helps make for a successful time together.

Don't try to do everything yourself

Create Rules and Routines

When you begin meeting, it's always a good idea to set some ground rules. For example, English Clubs usually have an "English only" rule. Naturally, students revert to speaking their native language when the topic gets complicated. Encourage them to stick with just speaking English. You may need to offer gentle "English only please…" reminders throughout the meeting to encourage them. Will people be allowed to drink and eat during the meeting? What about bringing a friend? Let the group participate in deciding the group rules. When new people come to the meeting be sure to fill them in on what is expected.

Who Can I Expect to Join my English Club?

You can invite anyone to join your English Club, including friends, family members, fellow students, co-workers, family members of visiting scholars, and people from other schools. English Clubs tend to be more fun when they are multigenerational and multicultural. If your best friend is joining, why not ask her grandmother to join, too? English Club members also work well when members have varying English language abilities. One member may be able to teach you something new, and another may benefit from a skill that you can share. Teaching someone else a grammar point or explaining how to use a new word is one of the best ways to review your skills.

Stop and Begin Again

Taking natural breaks throughout the year is a good idea. Some groups break for the summer months, but others may find that summertime is the perfect time to start a new group. Feel the rhythm of your campus and international culture and decide appropriately. Some colleges have international students arrive long before the semester begins to adjust to the culture. This might be the perfect time to gather a group of students since no classes are in session and students have more free time. Another good time to take a break is during holiday times, such as New Year's or Spring Break. Some members will return and others will move on to other things. Invite new people to join to fill the empty spots.

Change activities/themes that didn't work the first time. Keep adding new ideas, but try to maintain a club identity.

Use a Suggestion Box

If it's possible, keep a suggestion box in the room where you hold your club meetings. A bag or hat to pass around the tables is a good way to encourage members to write a comment or suggestion for the group. Examples of comments you might receive are: "I want to practice pronunciation more." or "Does anyone want to practice idioms with me?" "It's too cold in this room!" Someone might even suggest, "Why don't we all bring a snack to share next week?"

Offer Outings to the Group

Outside of your weekly meetings, it is a good idea to have one outing or excursion every month. This helps create stronger bonds within the group. It is always fun to have something to look forward to as well. Go out to a movie. Play a sport. Do community service together. Give blood. Go sightseeing. Have a picnic. Try that new Korean restaurant in town. Have a potluck dinner. Whatever you decide to do, everyone should speak English at all times.

Try Different Types of Curriculum

You can easily plan topics and conversations as you begin to meet. If you want some excellent help to go deeper, go online to find topics for conversation. Some like to use a curriculum from a group called Let's Start Talking. This group developed a Biblically-based curriculum where you can read through the book of Luke together and discuss the stories and their meaning. Friendspeak, the name of the curriculum, is being used throughout the United States in churches and campus ministries with wonderful results.

Watch to See God at Work

I met JeeYung at a conversation table at our local university. His bright and friendly smile caught my attention right away. We had only talked for a few minutes when he asked. *"Will you take me to church?"* I responded, *"Of course, I love to have you join us. I'll pick you up outside your dormitory main entrance at 10:15 on Sunday morning."* He was eager to grow closer to God during his time in the USA. We enjoyed many conversations over the next year. With internet video conferencing, we still stay in touch. I think back on those days and realize our friendship began at a table where we just wanted to hear each other's story ….in English.

Greg Swinney serves as the ministry facilitator for Crossroads International Student Ministries. International students have been a part of his life since 1984. Along with his wife, Laurie, they have great conversations around their kitchen table with students from all over the world.

Chapter 14

TRAVEL MINISTRY WITH INTERNATIONAL STUDENTS

by Dr. Bob Milliken

International students from Nebraska, July 2014

"Wayne"

"The Bible has never made sense to me," Wayne said with annoyance. Wayne and I sat in the back seat of a 12-passenger van, driving toward Estes Park, Colorado. We had traveled for three days, with three more days ahead of us. Wayne came to our state university from Taiwan to earn a Ph.D. in Physics. He was one of the top students in his department.

Wayne loved America, and his friends said even in Taiwan he seemed more American than Chinese. When he introduced himself to Americans he said, energetically, "My name is Wayne, like John Wayne." His wide, infectious smile always won people over. We had chosen him, along with five other top international students, for our leadership trip to Colorado after final exams.

"Maybe you should read it in Chinese," I suggested.

"That's even worse!" Wayne retorted, wrinkling his nose. "I understand it better in English. The Chinese translation is old and awkward!" His eyes flashed with energy, and his gelled black hair stood up for over an inch, like a fort above his forehead and ears. His stylish shirt and khaki shorts showed he was ready to hike!

This conversation led us to read the book of Jude

"Do you pray, and ask God to help you understand when you read?" I asked. "He promises in James 1:5 that he will gladly give wisdom to anyone who asks. He would certainly do that for those who want to understand His word."

This conversation led us to read the book of Jude, and discuss it verse by verse for the next hour, as the van labored up the Big Thompson canyon, and the other university students and sponsors chatted and looked out the windows at the rushing mountain stream and the steep rocky canyon walls. Tall green pines shone in the bright May sunshine. At the end of our hour of Bible study, Wayne exclaimed, "This is the first time the Bible has ever made sense to me!" We closed our study time in prayer.

"Lord," I prayed, "Thank You for Your Holy Word, which shows us how to live a life pleasing to you, and opens up to us the way of everlasting life. And thank you for opening our minds this afternoon, to understand Your word by Your Holy Spirit, in Jesus' name we pray, amen."

Wayne (3rd from right) on our
Student Leadership trip - May 2007

This conversation, made possible by the hours spent together in a van, and an acquaintance deepened by road-tripping, led to two years of weekly Bible study for Wayne and me. That August, Wayne was baptized into Jesus Christ. He became a leader for Christ on campus, and in his dorm. The following year he led his mother and sister to Christ. Now after his Ph. D. and a post-doc in Texas, he continues to influence others for Christ.

Wayne testifies at his baptism

My encounter with Wayne, in May 2007, illustrates the power of travel ministry to open doors of friendship and discipleship to international students. ISF (International Student Fellowship) has used travel ministry since its inception in Lincoln, Nebraska.

The Biblical Model

Travel Ministry: The Bible often demonstrates the power of travel ministry. When the Israelites left Egypt, they took with them a "mixed multitude" of other nations. They traveled together through the wilderness to the promised land (Exodus 12:38). Their shared experiences on the journey – the trials they endured together, many experiences of God's faithfulness, and the wonders they saw, brought many of these foreigners into the community of God's people. God prepared for their acceptance in His law which commanded Israel to treat foreigners the same as His people, promising foreigners the blessings of God's covenant people when they put their faith in Him (Exodus 12:48-49; Isaiah 56:3,6-8; 52:6).

The feasts of Israel also brought together God's people and converts from many nations. Luke's list of the people-groups at Pentecost (Acts 2:11) attests to the opportunity for spiritual transformation that resulted from these journeys.

People of many other nations also traveled to Israel, drawn by the renown of the LORD. Naaman (2 Kings 5), the Queen of Sheba (1 Kings 10), and the Magi (Matthew 2) illustrate this. Their interactions with God's people changed their lives.

In a similar way, Ling Lu traveled with ISF to a church two hours away to tell of her experience at the university and in the fellowship. Though not a believer, she got to spend the night with an American family, play with their children and their dog, experience Bible school and worship at the church the next day, her first time in a church service. She introduced herself to an attentive crowd and got to know some of the congregation during a delicious fellowship dinner after the service. A few weeks later she accepted an invitation by an ISF student to go to church with her. Just a few months later, she accepted Christ. The journey to the worship service played a pivotal role in helping her decide she could attend an American church service.

> *Just a few months later she accepted Christ*

Jesus' Method: Jesus' famous call embodies travel ministry: "Come, follow Me, and I will make you fishers of men" (Matthew 4:19). When Jesus chose His disciples, Mark tells us "He appointed twelve that they might be *with Him* and that He might *send them out* to preach and to have authority to drive out demons" (Mark 3:14-15, italics added). This expresses the essence of Jesus' model of discipleship, a pattern we should emulate in effective service to international students: 1) sharing life on the road, and 2) equipping those who believe for ministry.

Following Him meant you'd be on the move! You would usually get to sleep under the stars (Matthew 8:20). You would "be with Him" (Mark 3:14) and see how He handled every difficulty and challenge.

Traveling together builds bonds of shared meals, accommodations, hardships, new discoveries, and the unique ties of a team. Together in close quarters, whether walking dusty roads, or sitting in crowded vans for extended periods; these conditions break down psychological distance as well and often build life-long friendships. And when we purposely use such trips to help people build a relationship with Christ, road trips build the Kingdom of God, as Wayne's story shows so well. For example, consider Arun.

Arun

I met Arun, an Indian student working on his Ph. D. in Engineering, at an ISF Friday night dinner meeting. He was tall, slender, with dark eyes, dark black hair, and a broad smile. He loved conversation and showed a lively sense of humor and a broad knowledge of American culture gained from watching movies and television. He especially enjoyed *The West Wing*. When he heard I read and discussed the Bible with Wayne, he asked if we could do that. For the next 6 years we met each week to study books of the Bible - Mark, Revelation, Acts, Jonah, Romans, and on and on. Once or twice a week we would meet for epic 8-mile walks on the trails of our college town, talking over our lives, faith, and praying. We also took road trips to Omaha and Kansas City to visit art museums, to state parks for days of hiking, and occasionally overnight camping trips.

After six years of study, Arun accepted Christ and was baptized. For two months afterwards his mother, a university professor in India, called every night to talk him out of his new faith. "I can't argue with my mother, Bob," Arun lamented to me one evening as we hiked his favorite local trail. "She's too smart for me. I don't know what to say." But his deep conviction after years of consideration did not waver. Today he remains active in church in the city to which he moved for a job, participating in worship, Bible school, and service to the local homeless shelter.

Two summers ago Arun and I took a trip to Colorado – with his mother, who had come from India for her first visit to

America. We explored hot springs, waterfalls, high mountain trails, and saw much wildlife. We enjoyed many discussions of literature, culture, and religion. Arun and I shared the gospel with his mother, who listened thoughtfully, though skeptically. Yet, through that relationship his mother began reading the Gospel of John with me this summer.
Trips can build depths of ties and trust hard to develop elsewhere.

Aziz and Salma

I met Aziz and Salma at the weekly dinner put on by the international fellowship.

"We're from, Iran," Aziz said, responding to my questions. "I'm here on a research assistantship to support my Ph. D studies in engineering." Though Salma had an M.A. in Electrical Engineering from Iran, like her husband, she had not been given an assistantship, and could not afford to take classes.

We had many conversations about our home countries, and some about Islam and Christianity

As we chatted with those around the table, I learned Aziz enjoyed mountain climbing and had climbed many peaks in Iran. "Have you climbed in the U.S.A. also?" I asked.

"No, but I would like to," he replied, as he cut a piece of fried chicken with fork and knife.

He and his wife never returned to our dinner meetings, but that summer, when Salma returned to Iran for three months for family weddings, Aziz took four days away from his research duties to climb with me. We slept in tents in the forest at 10,000 feet and cooked over a camp stove. In three days we climbed six 14,000-foot peaks, including the two highest in the Rockies. We had many conversations about our two countries, and some about Islam and Christianity. When we returned Aziz studied the Gospel of Mark and John with me, and considered the claims of Jesus Christ. The trip together built the trust to be able to openly discuss our different faiths without feeling judged or condemned.

Aziz and I on Mt. Elbert in a blizzard, July 2015

Though Aziz and Salma have not come to Christ, we continue to share meals, go running, and take short trips together. This fall I took Aziz and Salma and one of their Iranian friends on a day-trip to our family farm in the Sandhills. Aziz cooked Iranian food for us over a campfire, we ran through the sandhills and swam in the clear waters of the Southfork of the Elkhorn River. We had many conversations about nature, God, and our dreams for the future. It excited me that my relationship with Aziz extended my influence into the life of his friend – on a trip! I pray the friendship we have forged may someday bring us all to share the same saving faith in Jesus Christ.

Types of Trips

Trips to serve international students come in limitless varieties and many purposes.

Cultural Awareness: Trips to art museums, historical sites, farms and ranches, museums, and state fairs all help international students understand America, and open channels for conversation.

Leadership trips: Each year International Student Fellowship of Lincoln, Nebraska selects students who show leadership potential and a commitment to Jesus. This trip helps us unify vision, set the spiritual tone for the coming year, plan activities, and deepen our roots in Christ. Time together in worship, study, and prayer helps us enjoy the Lord and each other, and find refreshment for our ministry.

Day trips: Day trips to Henry Doorly Zoo, bike trails, hiking trails, picnics, etc. introduce students to aspects of American life and culture, and help them find local activities they may enjoy on their own. Having enough volunteers along to build relationships with the international students and to answer questions increases the value of such trips.

We also offer trips to Walmart and grocery stores for students without transportation. Day trips deepen relationships developed on extended trips and keep contact with students who don't get involved with ministry activities.

Extended trips: Overnight trips take travel to another level and provide concentrated time together. Our trips range in length from one to 10 days and serve many purposes.

Conferences: Christmas break, 2013-2014 we took students to the Bridges Conference in Daytona Beach, Florida. Campus Crusade for Christ developed the Bridges conference to reach out in Jesus' name to international students. About half of the nine students we took were not believers, which the Bridges Conference recognized, offering tracks for non-believers. The lure of the beach (though it rained most of the time we were there!) brought many. But they knew they would experience a Christian environment. The high quality worship music and powerful speakers deeply impacted all of our students.

Dinner coming back from the Bridges Conference in Daytona Beach

Mission trips: Christian students need the opportunity to serve, and non-Christians can see another side of faith in Christ and the love of God they may not have considered before. These trips deepen the faith of believers and often bring just the touch non-believers need for their hearts to finally give in to the love of God.

Sight-seeing: Trips to major cities and national parks meet the desire of many international students to see as much of America as they can while studying here. ISF has had great success delighting students with well-run trips to top sights that build rich friendships and introduce some students to a saving relationship with Christ.

One-on-one trips: Some trips focus on just one or two people. I took my friend Michal, a Ph.D. student from Poland, on many afternoon or morning bike trips in our town. But this culminated in a weeklong trip to the mountains, climbing peaks, swimming in the hot springs, and whitewater rafting – all in the context of prayer, Bible study, and faith discussions.

One-on-one trips give ample opportunity for uninterrupted heart-to-heart discussions of spiritual matters, which some students would feel reluctant to share in more public settings.

Sometimes students bring visiting parents along.

Tips for Trips

1. **Safety:** Make sure you do all in your power to ensure the safety of students. Have proper insurance, bring first aid kits, and ensure that all drivers are experienced and reliable.

2. **Charge what trips cost:** International students tend to take trips more seriously when they invest in them. They seldom become no-shows when they register and pay in advance. Our ministry trips to Yellowstone and the Grand Canyon, though costing $500-800, usually cost hundreds of dollars less than those offered by commercial travel companies. And students usually prefer our trips. One Chinese Ph.D. student had taken a trip to Yellowstone the summer before with a noted local travel company, unaware that we offered a trip as well. On our Grand Canyon trip she said she wished she had gone with us. "Their trip didn't stay as long at sites I wanted to visit, and if we saw something interesting along the way that wasn't on the schedule, they wouldn't stop. Their trip cost more, and we saw less. The people weren't as friendly."

3. **Learn their language:** You can't learn every language, with students from scores of nations on campus. But you can learn some greetings and useful phrases from the nations going on your trip. Though the numbers may be different on your campus, the countries with the most students on U.S. campuses are China, India, Korea, Canada, Taiwan, and Japan. They total 56 percent of our international students!

4. **Learn about their cultures:** Study beforehand can help. But don't assume you understand. Let your research lead you to good questions you can ask. Let students explain their cultures. They will appreciate your interest and will enjoy helping you learn.

5. **Work for team unity:** Before the trip, and during it, emphasize Christian virtues like love, patience, unselfishness, and serving others. Most of our trips, even with non-Christians who did not know each other, have delighted us all with unity and mutual kindness. On one trip, two petite Chinese women, Ph. D. students, jumped out to wash our van

windows whenever we stopped for gas. "It's so fun!" they said, and we appreciated their help!

Emphasize that this is an opportunity to build life-long friendships through respect and understanding.

6. **Go the second mile:** You can't always please everyone, but you can try! Personalize the trip. Respond to requests, and present them to the group. They enjoy helping with trip decisions. Usually, they try to respect each other's wishes.

On our Grand Canyon trip, one student expressed an interest in seeing pictographs. We got online and found Newspaper Rock not far from our route. We stopped there and everyone enjoyed the fascinating, mysterious pictographs, still not deciphered by anthropologists!

7. **Arrange homestays with Christians along the way:** Seventy-five percent of international students never have an American friend or enter an American home. On our 9-day Grand Canyon trip, we stayed in homes three nights. Hospitality, time together with real Americans, and seeing how American family life works can have a profound impact on international students. And experiencing the love of ordinary Americans breaks down many stereotypes international students may come with.

8. **Don't be afraid to do the unique:** If you try to be creative, do so with qualified leaders and proper preparation. On our trips west we usually offer whitewater rafting, which the students rave about. On our Grand Canyon trip, three students chose to hike to the bottom and back, an exhausting 15-mile journey with 4400 feet of elevation gain. They praised it as among their favorite parts of the trip, a journey into the heart of God's Canyon.

9. **Don't hide your faith, be yourself:** Our Grand Canyon trip hosted eight international students; only two

knew Christ. We made it clear before the trip that ISF was a Christian organization, and that we would exhibit Christian morals and behavior. We prayed before every meal, had devotions each night, and attended Bible School and church on Sunday. These spiritual elements, the heart of our lives, sparked many discussions, and won the respect of all the students.

Make devotions short and of high quality, fun, devout, and sensitive to the needs of the students. All people long for love, and for eternal significance. Only Jesus satisfies these deepest needs.

10. Use Wilderness: As God led Israel into the wilderness, not by the main highway (Exodus 13:17-18), as crowds flocked to the wilderness to hear John the Baptist, as Jesus often taught away from the cities by the lake, on a mountain, or in the wilderness, we would be wise to emulate these examples. Teaching in nature, surrounded by the wonders of God's creation, adds a powerful witness of God's existence and love, that reinforces our teaching from the Bible.

Galileo and Isaac Newton, echoing Psalm 19, spoke of God's "Two Books" which reveal Him to us: Scripture and nature.

On the Grand Canyon trip (2016),

after our devotions "in the wilderness"

11. Spend time with every student: We make it a point to have significant conversations with every student during the trip. We ask about their families, about their work and research, about how life in America has been going, about their favorite foods, movies, books, places to visit, etc. Be a good listener! *Make sure you have enough American volunteers on every trip so every student experiences significant conversations and respect from an American.*

12. Be their friend even if they don't want to hear about Jesus: We don't appreciate people who only show interest in us if we might buy their product or share their views. God loves international students, and they need to know we value them, even if they don't share our faith.

Smile, invite them to sit with you at meals, ask them about their families, or places they enjoy visiting at home – let them know you care!

13. Work for the long term: Trust in God, love these precious students, and plant seeds of kindness and truth. Be ready to follow up with continuing relationships after the trips. It took six years for Arun to accept Jesus, but he has stood strong, and been a witness to others. A crop must grow to maturity before it can be harvested!

14. Pray! Our labors are for nothing if God does not give us insight and give open hearts in those we serve. Jesus urged us, "keep on praying, and don't give up!" (Luke 18:1), and "Ask, and it will be given you! .... Knock! The door will be opened!" (Matthew 7:7) Pray before and during the trip for God to move for salvation and true discipleship in us and our international guests.

15. Expect ecstasy! As the pictures show, travel to exciting places with people committed to God and to each other brings deep blessing and joy!

Jesus said, "Come away to a lonely place."

In June 2016, ISF took eight international students and visiting scholars on a nine-day trip to the Grand Canyon, and three other national parks and other major tourist destinations. We stayed with American host families three nights, attended Bible school and worshipped in Grand Junction, Colorado, and spent three days exploring the Grand Canyon. Three students hiked to the bottom of the canyon one day, an experience they will never forget. Each day an American leader gave a 10-15 minute devotional, presenting Jesus' love and the hope of heaven.

The sweet spirit of the students, the amazing natural wonders we saw, and the evidences of God's love made this trip unforgettable. Only two students began the trip as believers. Several students began attending Bible studies or going to church after the trip. One student accepted Christ a

After hiking into the heart of the Grand Canyon and back

month after the trip – partly due to the trip, and partly due to the influence of Wayne, mentioned in the beginning of this chapter. Wayne had invited Chung to the Chinese Church – a testimony to the continuing power of travel ministry for evangelism and discipleship, nine years after Wayne's baptism!

Spring Break With Astronauts!

Dai, a Ph.D. student in electrical engineering, joined ISF's annual Spring Break trip to Texas. He'd not participated with Christians before, but wanted to see more of America, and, as an engineer, the visit to the Space Center interested him. Twenty-four students and six American sponsors rode in two 15-passenger vans.

They stayed with American host families throughout the trip – three nights in Dallas and 3 in Houston. They attended a church service on Sunday, and enjoyed a fellowship dinner served by the church after worship. One evening after enjoying the Six Flags amusement park, they met local international students for a pot luck dinner put on by a church. After dinner the Texas international students shared testimonies of how they came to Christ which was very impressive to the Nebraska students, most of whom were not believers.

In Houston, they toured the Space Center. That night, after dinner, Dr. Dave, the director of astronaut training at the Space Center, gave a gripping talk. He presented over 200 slides showing the rigors of astronaut training and shared how he came to Christ, and how Jesus guided him in his work.

Dr. Dave's talk deeply affected Dai. Six months after the trip, he and five others from the trip accepted Christ and were baptized. Several others began attending church and Bible studies for the first time since arriving in America.

We have observed this pattern repeatedly! Travel attracts students who normally avoid Christian groups. The exposure to real Christians, the relationships they build, and the setting away from the pressures of school, allow them to rethink their preconceptions and begin to see the reality of God, and how a relationship with Him, through Jesus Christ, can fill life and eternity with purpose and joy. This often produces lifetime transformations.

As you see, travel ministry is fun, and opens many doors! Jesus modeled this when he said, "Come, follow Me!" We echo His call when we invite international students, "Come along with us!" With prayer and the Holy Spirit, the results often prove amazing!

Bob Milliken loves universities and the people who study there. He led a campus ministry at the University of Nebraska/Lincoln from 1978-1983. His teaching experience includes literature, writing, and theology at the University of Nebraska-Lincoln (1987-2006) and Nebraska Christian College (2006-2020). Bob has taught and preached at seminaries and churches on four continents. He's worked with international students for over 40 years. Bob is in his 19th year preaching at the Sidney (Iowa) Church of Christ. Bob and his wife Carol live in Lincoln, Nebraska.

Chapter 15

ANNOTATED CAMPUS MINISTRY RESOURCE LIST

by Dave Embree

Web Sites

Campus Ministry Resources

http://aofcm.org –Homepage of the Association of College Ministries, associated with Christian Churches and churches of Christ.

http://campusministry.org/ --Homepage of Campus Ministry Today which offers a number of resources for campus ministers, including their "Campus Ministry Toolbox".

http://www.campusrenewal.org/ --Campus Renewal seeks to build networks of churches and campus ministries and offers a variety of campus ministry resources including a free e-zine.

https://collegetransitioninitiative.com/ -- This is the college student-specific section of www.CPYU.org , the Center for Parent/Youth Understanding. These two linked sites/organizations are committed to helping parents and churches prepare students for the spiritual challenges of college.

https://collegeministry.com/ --Baptist student ministry site with resources for multiple structures of ministering to college students.

http://www.everystudent.com/ --Cru site that offers "a safe place to explore questions about life and God".

http://exploringcollegeministry.com/ --Encouraging and motivational blog by campus ministry researcher Benson Hines.

http://religion.ssrc.org/reforum/ --Essay Forum on the Religious Engagements of American Undergraduates. Exceptionally useful collection of academic articles relating to ministry to undergraduate students.

http://faithoncampus.com/blog/a-one-stop-list-of-college-ministry-resources/ --Excellent collection of resources for anyone doing campus ministry.

http://www.grassrootsfundraising.org/ --Grassroots Fundraising is a very practical site for principles and practices for resource raising.

http://www.heartsandmindsbooks.com/ --Website of a Pennsylvania bookstore founded by a former campus minister which provides exceptional book reviews and offers a huge selection of resources related to all aspects of campus ministry.

http://leaderu.com/ --Leadership U's archive and "hub" site for a variety of apologetic resources, associated with Cru.

https://www.youthworker.com/articles/?s=campus+ministry -- Youthworker Journal's collection of articles about campus ministry.

Home Pages for Campus Ministry Organizations

www.aofcm.org –Association of College Ministries, the campus ministries associated with non-denominational Christian churches.

http://www.chialpha.com/ --Assemblies of God campus ministries.

http://bcmlife.net/ --Baptist Collegiate Ministries—Southern Baptist Convention.

http://www.ccmanet.org/ --Catholic Campus Ministries.

http://campusforchrist.net/ --Churches of Christ (non-instrumental) campus ministries.

http://campusministryunited.com/ --Churches of Christ (non-instrumental) campus ministry organization focusing on outreach and training.

http://ccojubilee.org/ --Coalition for Christian Outreach; Reformed ministry serving schools in Indiana and east.

http://www.cru.org/ --CRU (formerly Campus Crusade for Christ). Largest campus ministry organization in the world.

http://destino.org/ --Destino is an outreach of CRU specifically targeted toward Latino students.

http://www.episcopalchurch.org/ministries/young-adult-and-campus-ministry --Episcopal Church campus ministry information hub.

https://www.elca.org/Our-Work/Related-Ministries/Campus-Ministry --Evangelical Lutheran Church in America campus ministry resources.

www.fca.org –Fellowship of Christian Athletes. An interdenominational Christian sports ministry to see the world impacted for Jesus Christ through the influence of athletes and coaches.

http://www.cmfi.org/whatwedo/globalscope/ --Home page for Globalscope, an international campus ministry planting arm of Christian Missionary Fellowship.

www.ifesworld.org –International Federation of Evangelical Students. Global fellowship of indigenous national Christian student movements.

https://intervarsity.org/ --InterVarsity Christian Fellowship. International campus ministry organization and source of many of the best resources available.

http://www.lcms.org/lcmsu --Lutheran Church Missouri Synod campus ministry hub.

http://www.campusministry.net/ --National Campus Ministers Association, an organization of "progressive" denominational campus ministries. Extensive archives of articles from a variety of sources about college students and spirituality.

https://www.navigators.org/Home --The Navigators. An international Christian outreach ministry with branches on many college campuses.

https://basiccm.org/about/ --Basic Campus Ministries is an organization that assists churches in developing effective outreach to college campuses in the Northeast, but their tools are useful to anyone doing church-based ministry anywhere.

www.ocf.net –Orthodox Christian Fellowship, a collaborative effort to shepherd and reach college students by the Orthodox Churches of America.

http://www.ruf.org/ --Presbyterian Church in America's Reformed University Fellowships home page (Biblically conservative).

https://www.presbyterianmission.org/ministries/collegiate/about-pcusa-collegiateyoung-adult-ministries/ --Presbyterian Church (USA) home base for campus ministry information.

www.ratiochristi.org --Ratio Christi (Latin for 'The Reason of Christ') is a global movement that equips university students and faculty to give historical, philosophical, and scientific reasons for following Jesus Christ.

www.stumo.org –Student Mobilization. Offshoot of Campus Crusade serving colleges in Arkansas, Missouri, Kansas, Colorado, Oklahoma and Texas.

https://www.younglife.org/ForEveryKid/YoungLifeCollege/Pages/Schools-with-Young-Life-College.aspx --Web center for Young Life's growing college component.

International Student Ministry Organizations and Resources

http://www.bridgesinternational.com/ --Bridges International is "a caring community of Christ-followers committed to serve, promote social connections and engage in spiritual conversations with international students so that students become leaders internationally", serving on many campuses across the US.

http://www.crossroadsinternational.net/ --Crossroads International Student Ministries. Exceptionally helpful resources on reaching out to and nurturing international students.

http://www.isionline.org/ --International Students, Inc. Considerable collection of resources through homepage of one of longest-term international student outreach organizations.

http://www.reachinginternationals.com/ --Helpful insights and tools for doing ministry with international students.

Significant Conferences Relating to Campus Ministry

https://catalystconference.com/ --Hub for everything related to Catalyst, an extensive set of gatherings and resources to help equip those dealing with young people.

http://theicom.org/ --Christian Church related missions conference held each November which offers some sessions geared specifically to college students.

www.aofcm.org –Mother site for Association of College Ministries which puts on retreats and conferences for campus ministers.

http://268generation.com/ --Access to everything you need to know about the massive Passion conference, which is aimed toward college students, held each January each year.

https://urbana.org/ --Homepage of InterVarsity's triennial huge missions conference geared towards college students, which, despite the name, is now held in St. Louis.
Insight into Campus Culture:

www.barna.org –Wealth of well-researched information on teens and young adults.

https://growingleaders.com/blog/?gclid=EAIaIQobChMIrKS3_bKl6wIVuymzAB2G2wykEAAYASABEgJu_PD_BwE – Tim Elmore's Growing Leaders blog. Helpful insights into what's going on with students and how we can best serve them.

http://chronicle.com/ --On-line version of the Chronicle of Higher Education, the leading professional journal related to colleges and universities.

http://www.sc.edu/fye/ --South Carolina University's National Resource Center for students' first year experiences.

http://www.heri.ucla.edu/ --UCLA's Higher Education Research Institute offering a wealth of studies regarding college students, including their annual report on that year's first-year students.

http://spirituality.ucla.edu/docs/reports/Spiritual_Life_College_Students_Full_Report.pdf --"The Spiritual Life of College Students: A National Study of College Students' Search for Meaning and Purpose" compiled by UCLA's HERI in 2003.

http://uwire.com/ --Sponsored press releases about issues related to college students.

Online Ezines and Communities for Students

http://www.boundless.org/ -- "Boundless is a community for Christian young adults who want to grow up, own their faith, date with purpose, and prepare for marriage and family."

http://www.lifeway.com/Collegiate/Summer-2013/c/N-1z13wmbZ1z104eb -- "Collegiate is an all-in-one resource designed with the contemporary look of a magazine and provides a refreshing combination of Bible study and feature articles centered on biblical truth and issues relevant to college students."

http://www.credomag.com/ --Theological and intellectual journal for Christian college students.

http://www.relevantmagazine.com/ --Online version of Relevant magazine, which addresses young adult faith and culture.

http://www.worldoncampus.com/ --World and national news related with a Christian perspective specifically for believing students.

Books

University Culture and Faith

The Resilience of Religion in American Higher Education by John Schmalzbauer and Kathleen A. Mahoney. Waco, TX: Baylor University Press, 2018. Despite many predictions through the years, religion is alive and well on the campuses of America, but where and why?

Cultivating the Spirit: How College Can Enhance Students' Inner Lives by Alexander W. Astin, Helen S. Astin, and Jennifer A. Lindholm. San Francisco: Jossey-Bass, 2010. Phenomenally well-researched study on the impact the university has on students' spiritual lives—has become an essential text in student life programs' understandings of their responsibilities regarding spirituality.

Finding God at Harvard: Spiritual Journeys of Thinking Christians by Kelly Monroe Kullberg. Downers Grove, IL: IVP, (revised) 2007—Ms. Kullberg's diligent search for living, practiced face at Harvard back in the 90's turned up far more serious Jesus-following than one might expect. Thoughtful, exemplary accounts.

Religion on Campus: What Religion really Means to Today's Undergraduates by Conrad Cherry, Betty A. DeBerg, and Amanda Porterfield. Chapel Hill and London: University of North Carolina Press, 2001. A scholarly look at what was happening with four distinct types of ministry on campus in four different parts of America at the beginning of the 21st century.

Professors Who Believe: The Spiritual Journeys of Christian Faculty by Paul M. Anderson. Downers Grove, IL: IVP, 1998—Though statistically University professors are the profession in America who have the lowest levels of belief and practice, many professors do believe, and their stories can be educational and influential for current students.

The Abandoned Generation: Rethinking Higher Education by William H. Willimon and Thomas H. Naylor. Grand Rapids, MI: Wm. B. Eerdmans Publishing Co., 1995. Brilliant insight as to how American higher education became so concerned about teaching the "right things" that student welfare got lost in the process.

The Secularization of the Academy by George Marsden and Bradley Longfield. London and New York: Oxford University Press, 1992. Thorough, but readable overview of the transformation of higher education in America from spiritual endeavor to secular tool.

Killing the Spirit: Higher Education in America by Page Smith. Penguin Books, 1990. An insider's critique of the "secular fundamentalism" inherent on modern university campuses.

The Closing of the American Mind: How Higher Education Has Failed Democracy and Impoverished the Souls of Today's Students by Allan Bloom. New York: Simon and Schuster, 1987—Classic work on how higher education has changed Americans' perspectives on "truth" and vice versa. Still worth reading.

A Christian Critique of the University by Charles Malik. Downers Grove, IL: IVP, 1982. A mind-expanding rethinking of the role that higher education plays in western culture and the Biblical imperative for the church to be actively involved.

The Messianic Character of American Education by Rousas John Rushdoony. Nutley, New Jersey: The Craig Press, 1979—Iconoclastic and extremely opinionated, Rushdoony still is effective in expositing the arc of philosophical progression in American higher education. Very useful for understanding how we have gotten to where we are.

History of Campus Ministry

God on Campus: Sacred Causes, Global Effects by Trent Sheppard. Downers Grove, IL: InterVarsity Press, 2009. More than just a history of spiritual awakenings on American university campuses, this book provides excellent insights into how godly students can choose to impact the colleges where they study.

Campus Ministry: Restoring the Church on the University Campus by Douglas A. Dickey. Joplin, MO: College Press, 1994. A visionary leader and innovator among Christian Church campus ministries, Doug Dickey took it upon himself to write a historical overview of this group of ministries.

Inquiring and Discerning Hearts: Vocation and Ministry with Young Adults on Campus by Sam Portaro and Gary Peluso. Scholars Press, 1993. Overview of the development and impact of mainline denominational campus ministries in America since 1948.

Campus Ministry in the Coming Age by Thomas R. McCormick. St. Louis: CBP Press, 1987. A history of Disciples of Christ efforts to reach out to college students until 1986, with a concluding chapter on what challenges were facing mainline church campus ministries in the late 80's.

Forgotten Christians: A Guidebook for College-Career Work by Charles Garrison. Joplin, Missouri: College Press, 1967. Early Christian Church publication about why campus ministry matters.

A Brief History of the International Fellowship of Evangelical Students edited by Douglas Johnson. Lausanne: I.F.E.S and Intervarsity Press, 1964—On the way to telling the story of the IFES itself, a brief but comprehensive account of the church's outreach efforts on the university campus is recounted.

The Great Awakening at Yale College edited by Stephen Nissenbaum. Belmont, CA: Wadsworth Publishing Company, 1972—A fascinating and insightful collection of documents of the impact of the First Great Awakening on the students of Yale.

Conscience on Campus: An Interpretation of Christian Ethics for College Life by Waldo Beach. New York: Association Press, 1958—It is seldom noted that the first groups to do widespread non-denominational campus ministry were the Young Men's and Women's Christian Associations; this slim volume demonstrates the deep thinking and careful intention practiced by the campus "Y" movement.

Two Centuries of Christian Student Movements: Their Origin and Intercollegiate Life by Clarence P. Shedd. New York: Association Press, 1934; and A Century of Christian Student Initiative by Clarence P. Shedd. New York: Association Press, 1945. These two older volumes contain incredibly detailed and insightful material about Christian student movements in the academic "dark ages".

Attributes and Needs of College Students

Generation Z Unfiltered by Tim Elmore and Andrew McPeak. Atlanta: Poet Gardener Publishing, 2019—Data-driven research that gives significant insight into what Gen Z is all about and how to connect with them effectively.

Faith for Exiles by David Kinnamon and Mark Matlock. Grand Rapids, MI: Baker Books, 2019. Insightful, hopeful, practical. If you are only going to read one book about leading Gen Z to spiritual maturity, make it this one.

The New Copernicans: Millennials and the Survival of the Church by David John Seel Jr. Nashville: Thomas Nelson Publishers, 2018. Yes, we are past Millennials and well into Generation Z, but the same forces that have shaped Millennials are still at work.

Marching Off the Map: Inspire Students to Navigate a Brand New World by Tim Elmore and Andrew McPeak. Atlanta: Poet Gardener Publishing, 2017. Yes, Gen Z really is different from every previous generation. What makes these "digital natives" so unique.

Churchless: Understanding Today's Unchurched and How to Connect with Them edited by George Barna and David Kinnamon. Carol Stream, IL: Tyndale Momentum, 2014. Since younger people tend to be less connected with the church than ever before, the Barna team's insights are especially significant to those doing campus ministry.

Visions of Vocation by Steve Garber. Downers Grove, IL: InterVarsity Press, 2014. Though not all will preach or lead worship, all are called to be salt and light in this world, through whatever means God puts before them; this work gives great insight into how to talk with others about fulfilling their calling.

Every Good Endeavor: Connecting Your Work to God's Work by Timothy Keller. New York: Penguin Books, 2014. Keller articulates well the concept that "vocation" (calling from God) takes many forms, but all have common goals. This is an excellent book to take soon-to-be-graduating students through.

Playing God: Redeeming the Gift of Power by Andy Crouch. Downers Grove, IL: Intervarsity Press, 2013. Crouch notes that though humans often see power as a problem, that God has given it to humans as a tool to be used for His glory. University students become among the most powerful people in any culture, and this book helps understand and direct that power.

Spiritual Formation in Emerging Adulthood: A Practical Theology for College and Young Adult Ministry by David P. Setran and Chris A. Kiesling. Grand Rapids: Baker Academic, 2013. Combining social science research with

Biblical truth, the authors offer many insights into the unique challenges and opportunities facing the age group which includes college students, and provides practical suggestions on how to help these young people spiritually mature.

Shaping the Journey of Emerging Adults: Life-Giving Rhythms for Spiritual Transformation by Richard R. Dunn and Jana L. Sundene. Downers Grove, IL: IVP, 2012. A guide on how to effectively use the process of relationship-building (rather than a written curriculum) to foster spiritual growth in young adults.

You Lost Me: Why Young Christians are Leaving Church and Rethinking Faith by David Kinnamon. Grand Rapids, MI: BakerBooks, 2011--Why do so many "church kids" wander away while they're in college? This volume looks at causes and responses.

Lost in Transition: The Dark Side of Emerging Adulthood by Christian Smith, Kari Christoffersen, Hilary Davidson, and Patricia Snell Herzog. London: Oxford University Press, 2011. Based on interviews and other research, this book looks at the major factors effecting "prolonged adolescence" and "none of the above" spiritual perspectives and calls for a "realistic concern" approach to addressing them.

Generation iY: Our Last Chance to Save their Future by Tim Elmore. Atlanta: Poet Gardener Publishing, 2010—Elmore examines how the internet and especially social media have impacted later-born millennials and offers specific tips regarding effective communication with them.

Souls in Transition: The Religious and Spiritual Lives of Emerging Adults by Christian Smith and Patricia Snell. London: Oxford University Press, 2009. Written as a follow-up to Soul Searching this book is based on the same objective social science research tools and reveals a remarkably more complex interaction between "emerging adults" and religious ideas.

The First Year Out: Understanding American Teens after High School by Tim Clydesdale. Chicago: University of Chicago Press, 2007. Clydesdale studies college students and their faith. This book gives useful insight into their desire to experience new freedoms without totally giving up their heritage and how "sticky" that can be.

Soul Searching: The Religious and Spiritual Lives of American Teenagers by Christian Smith with Melinda Lundquist Denton. London: Oxford University Press, 2005. Amazingly broad study of what teens were believing and doing in the first decade of the 2000's; much of the underlying thinking among teens has remained fairly constant.

Spiritual but not Religious: Understanding Unchurched America by Robert C. Fuller. New York: Oxford University Press, 2001—Predating the wave of self-identifying "nones" among college students, Fuller looks at the trends in America regarding allegiance to faith communities, and the consequences of people's disassociations.

Practical Campus Ministry

Disruptive Witness: Speaking the Truth in a Distracted Age by Alan Noble. Downers Grove, IL: InterVarsity Press,

2018. How do you get the attention of people who are hypnotized by electronic devices and getting thousands of messages daily from others?

Campus Ministry: Restoring the Church on the University Campus, by Doug Dickey and updated by Greg Swinney. Kearney, NE: Lifechange Media, 2013. Veteran campus minister Greg Swinney passionately shares practical insights into building up young believers on the University campus.

College & University Chaplaincy in the 21st Century: A Multifaith Look at the Practice of Ministry on Campuses across America edited by Dr. Lucy A. Forster-Smith. SkyLight Paths, 2013. Individuals from a wide variety of backgrounds who are actively engaged in the increasingly rare role of "chaplain" explore the practice, theology and joys of campus ministry and the chaplain's calling to support, challenge, stir the imagination of and address this generation's urgent longing for connection and meaning.

College Ministry in a Post-Christian Culture by Stephen Lutz. The House Studio, Sep 1, 2011. The key word to this book is "missional". Lutz laments that many campus ministers are caught up in antiquated ideas about college ministry, which often focus more on "gathering" than "sending". The author gives plenty of suggestions regarding developing ministries that DO instead of just talking about it

College Ministry from Scratch: A Practical Guide to Start and Sustain a Successful College Ministry, by Chuck Bomar. Grand Rapids: Zondervan/Youth Specialties, 2010. This book, written by the leading voice in local-congregation-based college-age ministry, offers tons of practical insights into how to grow such students up into spiritual adulthood.

Campus Renewal: A Practical Plan for Uniting Campus Ministries in Prayer and Mission by Justin Christopher. Austin: Campus Renewal Ministries, 2010. Insight into bringing the ministries on any campus together into campus-impacting unity.

College Ministry 101: A Guide to Working with 18-25 Year Olds by Chuck Bomar. Grand Rapids: Zondervan/Youth Specialties, 2009. This volume addresses the philosophical framework for why college ministry is vital to the local church.

Reaching the Campus Tribes by Benson Hines (free ebook available at http://reachingthecampustribes.com/), 2009. Reflections on an entire year spent visiting campus ministries across America, and practical insights based on that journey.

Reach the U: A Handbook for Effective Campus Ministry edited by Dennis Gaylor. Springfield, MO: Chi Alpha Campus Ministries, USA, 2003. A compendium about many different aspects of campus ministry all written by "veterans" of campus work.

The Fuel and the Flame: 10 Keys to Ignite Your College Campus for Jesus Christ by Steve Shadrach. Authentic Media, 2003. Shadrach, who founded Student Mobilization in 1986, emphasizes the attributes needed in someone who is going to effectively do ministry on campus (the "fuel") and then addresses means to impact individual students and to build communities of believers on campus (the "flame").

Shaping the Spiritual Life of Students: A Guide for Youth Workers, Pastors, Teachers & Campus Ministers by Richard R. Dunn. Downers Grove, IL: Intervarsity Press, 2001. Campus ministers want to impact students' lives; this book gives insight into how.

Getting Real: An Interactive Guide to Relational Ministry by Ken Baugh and Rich Hurst. Colorado Springs, CO: Navpress, 2000—Comprehensive guide to ministering to young adults. A bit dated, but still very insightful and practical.

Spiritual Mentoring: A Guide to Seeking and Giving Direction by Keith R. Anderson and Randy D. Reese. Downers Grove, IL: IVP, 1999. By now, a classic and fairly comprehensive guide to creating and maximizing mentoring relationships.

Ministering in the Secular University: A Guide for Christian Professors and Staff by Joseph McRae Mellichamp. Carrollton, TX: Lewis and Stanley, 1997. Believing faculty and staff often walk a fine line between not using the roles they have to impact students and doing/saying too much in ways that endanger their roles. This volume helps committed, caring faculty and staff to find the proper, joyful and effective balance.

Taking Education Higher: An Equipping Manual for Ministry on the University Campus edited by Greg Swinney. Kearney, NE: Lifechange Media, 1993. A compilation of chapters written by people earnestly engaged in representing Christ on campus.

Ministering to Students Through the Church, compiled by Art Herron. Nashville: Convention Press, 1989. Good basic introduction to the challenges of reaching out to college students from a local congregation with some good insights into how to do it effectively.

Campus Ministry Structures and Fund Raising

Fundraising Freedom: 7 Steps to Build and Sustain Your Next Campaign by Mary Valloni. Powell, OH: Author Academy Elite, 2016. Ms. Valloni is a campus ministry alumna who often consults with campus ministries on fund-raising (especially capital projects) and helps with training for individual fund-raising.

The God Ask: A Fresh, Biblical Approach to Personal Support Raising by Steve Shadrach. CMM Press, 2013. Many campus ministers have been using Shadrach's principles and finding much success in so doing.

Raising More than Money: Redefining Generosity Reflecting God's Heart by Doug M. Carter. Nashville, TN: Thomas Nelson, 2007—Campus ministers need advocates and funding, and this book provides practical steps to building both.

Funding Your Ministry by Scott Morton. NavPress, 2007. This book has been specifically recommended by campus ministers as effective.

Friend Raising: Building a Missionary Support Team That Lasts by Betty J. Barnett. YWAM Publishing, 2002. Few campus ministers enjoy fund-raising, but tend to be good at building relationships. This book describes how doing the latter can accomplish the former.

Building Effective Boards for Religious Organizations: A Handbook for Trustees, Presidents, and Church Leaders, edited by Thomas P. Holland and David C. Hester. San Francisco: Jossey-Bass Publishers, 2000. Older collection of essays on getting disparate groups of people to focus effectively on the same goals.

Doing Good Better! How to be an Effective Board Member of a Nonprofit Organization by Edgar Stoesz and Chester Raber. Intercourse, PA: Good Books, 1997. Boards can be the functioning foundations of campus ministries or dead weight ministers have to facilitate and endure. This book gives suggestions to enable the former.

Campus Outreach

aka "Lost": Discovering Ways to Connect with the People Jesus Misses Most by Jim Henderson. Colorado Springs: Waterbrook Press, 2005. Enabling believers to transition from seeing evangelism as "weird and scary" to "a normal part of daily Christian life" is the intention and impact of this book.

Generating Hope: A Strategy for Reaching the Postmodern Generation by Jimmy Long. Downers Grove, IL: IVP, 1997. A bit dated, but good insight into communicating the unchanging truth of the Gospel in ways accessible to post-moderns.

More Ready than You Realize: Evangelism as Dance in the Postmodern Matrix by Brian McLaren. Grand Rapids, MI: Zondervan, 2002. Helpful primer on meeting people where they are to communicate the Gospel.

Godspace: Where Spiritual Conversations Happen Naturally by Doug Pollock. Loveland, CO: Group Publishing, 2009—Innovative introduction to conversational/story-telling approaches to sharing one's faith.

Evangelism Outside the Box: New Ways to Help People Experience the Good News by Rick Richardson. Downers Grove, IL: IVP, 2000—Why do we tend to have a few dozen leaders "running" our own ministries and maybe have two or three outreach leaders to take on our campuses of thousands? That's one of the boxes we need to escape. There are more and this book helps us understand what they are and how to proceed.

Reimagining Evangelism: Inviting Friends on a Spiritual Journey by Rick Richardson. Downers Grove, IL: IVP, 2006—Not even the slightest hint of "evangelism program" but rather a relationship-based approach to authentically sharing one's faith.

Revolution: Effective and Personal Evangelism by Jay Strack. Nashville: Nelson Impact, 2006. Innovative study guide/workbook for working through both the "why's" and "how's" regarding students sharing their faith on campus.

Campus Evangelism Handbook: A Practical Guide for Showing and Sharing God's Love edited by Andres Tapia.

Downers Grove, IL: IVP, 1987. Dated volume, but still plenty of practical advice.

Campus Ministry and World Missions

Student Power in World Missions by David M. Howard. Downers Grove, IL: IVP, 1979. Insightful and motivational overview of the history of student interest and involvement in world evangelism with special emphasis on the Student Volunteer Movement and Student Foreign Missions Fellowship.

Resources for Students

Welcome to College: A Christ-Follower's Guide for the Journey by Jonathan Morrow. Kregel Publications, 2017. A guide to the questions that arise during every day of one's college experience, from "Why believe in God?" to "How do I deal with the hook-up scene in college?"

CAMPUS gODS: Exposing the Idols That Can Derail Your Present and Destroy Your Future by Guy Chmieleski. Franklin, TN: Seedbed Publishing, 2013. College is not about "to believe or not to believe", it is about WHAT will someone believe. Chmielseski gives some direction on sorting through the various options on campus.

King of the Campus by Stephen Lutz. The House Studio, 2013—Easily readable, enjoyable introduction to college life with very specific advice on how to do college spiritually well.

Campus Voices: A Student to Student Guide to College Life, written by college students; compiled by Paul Buchanan and Paula Miller. Ventura, CA: Regal, 2009. Dozens of short essays by students on how to do college well, with a focus on the spiritual.

Student to Student: A Guide to College Life, written by college students; compiled by Paul Buchanan and Paula Miller. Ventura, CA: Regal, 2007. Advice on living faithfully amidst the challenges of "college world."

Brown Like Coffee: For Students Who Think Outside the Box by Steve Shadrack. The Bodybuilders Press, 2007—Down-to-earth guide to campus life and how to stay on track spiritually.

Can You Keep Faith in College? by Abbie Smith. Multnomah Press, 2006. Advice from over 50 Christian students on how to not only survive, but to thrive during their college years. Covers many elements of campus life.

University of Destruction: Your Game Plan for Spiritual Victory on Campus by David Wheaton. Minneapolis: Bethany House, 2005. Very socially and politically conservative, but realistic in its portrayal of the dangers facing any incoming student with some practical advice for not getting "sucked into" the usual campus culture.

How to Stay Christian in College: An Interactive Guide to Keeping the Faith by J. Budziszewski. Colorado Springs: Navpress, 1999. Still a remarkably multi-faceted tool to assist students in remaining faithful during their college years which even offers additional readings on topics which interest students.

Following Jesus in the "Real World": Discipleship for the Post-College Years by Richard Lamb. Downers Grove, IL: IVP, 1995. When students graduate, suddenly they are "freshmen in the real world." This book can help send them out more prepared to thrive spiritually apart from their college fellowships.

The Complete Campus Companion: The Survival Guide Every Christian Student Needs edited by Robert M. Kachur. Downers Grove, IL: IVP, 1988. Somewhat dated, but dozens of solid chapters about many aspects of student life. No chapters on internet porn or Facebook defriending, but helpful info on topics as diverse as how to survive the divorce of one's parents and what makes a career "Christian."

Special thanks to **Dave Embree** who compiled this helpful list of resource materials.